More Praise for *Toxic Inequality*

"In *Toxic Inequality*, Thomas M. Shapiro shows that inequality harms everyone—that it squanders talents, misallocates resources, and suppresses initiative. Deftly blending facts and figures with moving personal stories, this book reveals how severe inequality is, why it matters, and what we can do about it."

—GEORGE LIPSITZ, author of
The Possessive Investment in Whiteness

"*Toxic Inequality* calls it like it is. People of color and low-income communities are ensnarled in a web of poisonous economic disparities and structural racial inequities that prevent wealth-building, erode home ownership, limit education and job possibilities, and stall mobility. Based on extensive interviews, Thomas M. Shapiro and his team portray those who, despite their struggle to succeed, continue to fall behind. Eliminating this toxic inequality requires a sustained and systemic assault on the policies that have created and perpetuate this injustice. This timely book reveals the cure: just and fair inclusion into a society in which all can participate, prosper, and achieve their full potential—equity."

—ANGELA GLOVER BLACKWELL, CEO, PolicyLink

TOXIC
INEQUALITY

TOXIC INEQUALITY

How America's Wealth Gap
Destroys Mobility, Deepens the Racial Divide,
& Threatens Our Future

THOMAS M. SHAPIRO

BASIC BOOKS

NEW YORK

Published in the United States by Basic Books, an imprint of Perseus Books, LLC, a subsidiary of Hachette Book Group, Inc.

Books published by Basic Books are available at special discounts for bulk purchases in the United States by corporations, institutions, and other organizations. For more information, please contact the Special Markets Department at Perseus Books, 2300 Chestnut Street, Suite 200, Philadelphia, PA 19103, or call (800) 810-4145, ext. 5000, or e-mail special.markets@perseusbooks.com.

Designed by Linda Mark

Library of Congress Cataloging-in-Publication Data
Names: Shapiro, Thomas M., author.
Title: Toxic inequality : the true costs of poverty and racial injustice
    for America's families / Thomas M. Shapiro.
Description: New York : Basic Books, [2017] | Includes bibliographical
    references and index.
Identifiers: LCCN 2016043570 (print) | LCCN 2016058087 (e-book) |
    ISBN 9780465046935 (hardcover : alk. paper) |
    ISBN 9780465094875 (e-book)
Subjects: LCSH: Poverty—United States. | Income distribution—
United States. | Equality—United States. | Racism—United States. |
    United States—Economic conditions—21st century. | United
    States—Social conditions—21st century.
Classification: LCC HC110.P6 S43 2017 (print) | LCC HC110.P6
(ebook) | DDC 339.4/60973—dc23
LC record available at https://lccn.loc.gov/2016043570

10 9 8 7 6 5 4 3 2 1

For Ruth and Izak,
The wealth of my life

CONTENTS

Introduction

DREAMS DEFERRED
AND DERAILED

PATRICIA ARRORA'S STORY COULD HAVE TAKEN MANY TURNS. The daughter of a single mom who worked as a maid until she became disabled, Patricia grew up in the crime- and drug-plagued neighborhood of Watts, in South Central Los Angeles. At an early age, she became a single mother herself and began collecting welfare benefits. But although Watts's troubles defined Patricia's early years, a desire to move up and away from her hometown's ills—its bad reputation, its gangs, and its drugs—motivated her subsequent life's journey. Despite challenges and detours along the way, she has secured many of her dreams. But her path was harder than it had to be. For African American single moms like her, and for many other Americans, barriers to prosperity are too high to overcome through individual achievement, and success is rarer than it should be.

My colleagues and I first met Patricia in 1998, when she was forty-six years old. Hers was one of 187 families across the United States that we interviewed in hopes of learning how differing wealth resources shape the plans, opportunities, and futures of individuals from different walks of life. We wanted to understand how people chose schools for their children, decided where to live to best accommodate their family's needs, and planned to achieve economic mobility. We were also eager to learn about the different pathways that lower-income families and families of color must take as they strive for better lives.

We recruited families from child-care centers and through word of mouth in Boston, Los Angeles, and St. Louis. By design, about half of the families we interviewed were white, and half were African American; half were middle-class or better-off, and half were working-class or poor; half resided in the three cities themselves, and half lived in suburbs of those same metropolitan areas. From the interviews we conducted in the late 1990s, we gleaned invaluable insights into the hopes, dreams, and difficulties of a wide swath of American families.[1] But we learned far more when we checked back with these families over a decade later.*

Between 1998 and 2010, when we conducted our first follow-up interviews, the Great Recession and implosion of

---

* The appendix provides a fuller description of our study's sample and methodology, mentioning that we changed the names and other identifying characteristics of the people profiled in this book and that they were compensated for their participation.

the US housing market hit hard. Beginning in late 2007 and officially ending in mid-2009, this crisis profoundly impacted families nationwide. In the wake of the recession, between 2010 and 2012, the team contacted and interviewed 137 of the 187 families interviewed twelve years before. Technically speaking, the recession was over, but our conversations revealed that the crisis was clearly still unfolding. Most of the families we talked with were reeling from job losses, adjusting to reduced incomes, or having trouble making mortgage payments. One adult in fifty-three of the families had lost his or her job during the recession; fifty families experienced lower incomes at some point during the recession; and at least a dozen had fallen behind on their mortgages. Seven families lost their homes due to foreclosure.

By 2012, those who had been children when we conducted our first set of interviews were now young adults finishing high school, planning for college, entering the workforce, or starting families of their own. The parents we spoke to in 1998 were now in a position to tell us how their plans had worked out and how their resources had affected their own mobility and that of their children. With these two sets of interviews in hand, we traced the divergent advantages and challenges associated with race and economic status that confront families striving to move ahead in the United States. The interviews underlined how we must understand economic and racial inequality in tandem, how vast wealth disparities and racial injustice do real harm to individual families, and how powerful institutional forces, rather than individual choices, distinguish those families who get ahead from those stuck in place or falling behind. The story of Patricia and her family illustrates many of these themes and exemplifies the political and economic structures that at times helped launch her economic mobility and at others destroyed her wealth.

When we first talked to Patricia Arrora at her apartment in 1998, she had just moved herself off of social assistance. She and 13 million other people had been receiving cash assistance when the program known as Aid to Families with Dependent Children (AFDC) ended in 1996. Subsequent economic growth pulled her and others from welfare into paying jobs and by 2000 had, along with new rules restricting eligibility for social assistance, halved the rolls in the program that replaced AFDC, Temporary Assistance for Needy Families. When we spoke Patricia had taken a job processing applications for a local utility company in Los Angeles County, and the probationary salary put her family's income just below the federal government's official poverty threshold. This threshold is the minimum level of income deemed adequate to feed, clothe, and house a family; it is calibrated by family size. The calculation is based on this standard, as is eligibility for some government programs. For Patricia's family of three in 1998 the poverty line was $13,650. Patricia wistfully told us that she was looking to meet a millionaire to rescue her. Still, if she succeeded past the probationary period and secured a permanent position, the annual pay of $19,800 (in 1998 dollars) would nudge Patricia and her four- and five-year-old daughters just above the poverty line. A job paying less than $20,000 a year may not sound like much, and Patricia had no financial wealth: no savings, stocks, bonds, property, or car, and certainly no pension or other retirement plan. But for Patricia, the job represented a huge and proud step up.

Sitting in her apartment in 1998, Patricia told us how she had taken classes to learn computer skills, gaining experience that paved the road away from AFDC and helped her secure employment. Having a job and knowing that tomorrow would bring a stable, earned paycheck was crucial to Patricia's identity and dignity. Although eager to bring home more than the $700 monthly welfare payments she had been receiving, she also longed for the sense of self-esteem that came with work. Some critics view poor people as suffering from character defects, such as a lack of ambition or work ethic, welfare dependence, or an inability to defer gratification. Patricia didn't actually have these traits.

In addition to work and money, housing and community were constant concerns in Patricia's life. In 1998, she was living in subsidized rental housing in West Los Angeles, fourteen miles west of Watts, a neighborhood that offered too many traumatic reminders of where she had grown up. Patricia feared the menacing guys who hung out on the nearby street corner. She hoped to buy a home in a safe, welcoming community where her daughters could thrive—a winning, and very American, plan.

Our interview with Patricia in 2010 revealed that she had made good on that plan, but not without great struggle. In 2003, she purchased a home in a different neighborhood in West LA with the assistance of the Family Self-Sufficiency program of the Department of Housing and Urban Development (HUD). Residents living in public housing or receiving rent subsidies pay 30 percent of their income for rent and utilities. Increases in work income get siphoned off by higher rent, which potentially creates a work disincentive. The program permits families receiving rental subsidies to place in escrow the rent increases that usually accompany increased earnings, enabling families to simultaneously increase their earned income and to save money to improve their lives. Patricia used the escrowed monies as a down payment on a home. The new neighborhood featured open spaces, greater safety, and comparatively high-quality schools. But the community still reminded her of Watts. Even though her family was moving up, Patricia was not happy with what she described as a "drug-infested, gang area." She recalled a couple of incidents in which gangs had approached relatives, making the family reluctant to venture out to neighborhood stores. Despite precautions, their house was robbed. She "felt violated," and the "kids didn't want to sleep in their bedrooms. . . . They were afraid." It was time to move again.

In 2006, Patricia leveraged first-time home ownership with equity built up in Los Angeles's hot housing market to buy a larger, brand-new home sixty miles away in Los Angeles's Inland Empire exurbs (Riverside and San Bernardino counties). Shortly thereafter, however, the housing crisis and the Great Recession wreaked havoc on the family's hard-earned success and imperiled Patricia's plans for her children's future. In 2010, some two years after the crisis, we sat down with Patricia in the kitchen of her Riverside-area home. She now earned a middle-class income of $50,000 annually and had financial assets amounting to $7,000, putting her family above the asset poverty line—the minimum amount of wealth needed to keep a family out of poverty for three months. Her family had expanded as well. Patricia had married Frank in 2003. After working for years at a good union job, Frank had been unemployed since 2008, and he was still collecting unemployment. His inability to contribute financially to the household was a source of family tension.

Patricia was happy with her home. She described how she took equity built up in her first home in West LA, gave a large sum to her mother and other kin to help them out, and used the rest to put a $112,000 down payment on the new home. Yet, the housing crisis hit hard and not all was right financially. The balance Patricia owed on her mortgage exceeded the home's plummeting value. The loan terms prohibited her from refinancing. With her husband out of work, she was struggling to make mortgage payments on one income, and she had entered a government-sponsored loan modification program. Patricia was stuck paying other bills on credit cards.

And although pleased with her home, Patricia was unhappy with the neighborhood high school, which she described as "run down . . . dirt." The school's test scores, well below California's average, corroborate Patricia's observation. Reflecting area demographics, 96 percent of the high school's students are youths of color, and nearly three-quarters qualify for subsidized lunches because they come from families with incomes 185 percent below the poverty line.[2] So Patricia enrolled her girls, Brittany and Brianna, in a different high school fifteen miles from their new home. Both girls ran track and hoped to go to college. One had a 3.5 GPA and expected to go to a state college on a scholarship. The other struggled with juvenile diabetes, which had compromised her energy and ability to concentrate, and her GPA hovered around 2.0. Patricia had told the girls that because she couldn't afford to take on any additional debt, they would have to get scholarships and financial aid to continue their education.

Patricia liked the quiet and safety of her subdivision, but she worried she had made a mistake moving somewhere so isolated from public transportation. Patricia drove the girls twenty minutes to their high school, which was out of her way; because she would also have to drive them to any part-time job they might find, they were effectively unable to work. The girls wanted a car to get around, but Patricia was unable to afford one or the added insurance, so she insisted they ride the bus. For the girls' benefit, she attempted to use the situation to teach some difficult lessons, telling them that she had come up hard and that they must pay for their own transportation, "because it won't be coming out of my pocket."

Overrun by foreclosures during and after the crisis, Patricia's subdivision was changing rapidly around her. During our interview she estimated that at least ten houses were on the market in the neighborhood at that moment, and I noticed "for sale" signs on about every third house, with dried-up and unkempt lawns throughout the neighborhood. People were just "walking away from their houses," Patricia reported. She had been especially fond of one neighboring family, but when they couldn't afford to make their payments, they left. Within one mile of Patricia's home, sixty-eight families lost homes due to foreclosure between 2008 and early 2013. Indeed, Patricia's subdivision illustrates the broad destruction of family wealth in the Inland Empire, where 54.9 percent of home owners owed more on their mortgages than the homes' value in late 2009; by early 2013, 35.7 percent were still "underwater." In recent years, Wall Street investment firms have issued securities and amassed billions in funding to buy foreclosed homes. In March 2013, for instance, investors bought up 57.8 percent of the Inland Empire homes made available through the foreclosure process before they ever reached the open market.[3]

The high number of foreclosures in the neighborhood was not a matter of chance. KB Home, purveyors of the American dream, had developed Patricia's subdivision. KB's gated master-planned communities, located throughout the Inland Empire, feature swimming pools, walking trails, tot lots, and parks.[4] KB also connects potential buyers to financial services, which is how so many buyers in Patricia's neighborhood came to get mortgages from Countrywide Financial Corporation. One of the biggest mortgage lenders in the Inland Empire, Countrywide also became the poster child for predatory lending. In 2015, in a $335 million settlement with the US Department of Justice, Countrywide stipulated that it had discriminated against more than 200,000 African American and Hispanic borrowers between 2004 and 2008, steering them toward subprime loans and charging higher fees and interest rates, even though those borrowers had credit profiles similar to white borrowers who received prime loans.[5] Patricia was one of those borrowers. She felt cheated by the terms of her mortgage; by the close relationships between KB Home, the mortgage appraisers, and Countrywide; and by a large "hidden" fee that unexpectedly appeared at the closing. Such fees were a part of Countrywide's business model because it was a mortgage machine with subsidiaries providing services and extracting fees throughout loan applications, lending, and servicing. In a separate settlement, the

Federal Trade Commission determined that Countrywide had bilked 450,000 customers by overcharging on services, even charging some borrowers whose homes were in foreclosure $300 to mow their lawns. Countrywide paid the Federal Trade Commission a settlement fine of over $1 million. Like Countrywide, KB Home settled several class-action lawsuits related to its practices, stipulating that it had approved loans to borrowers who were not eligible, approved loans based on overstated or incorrect income, failed to include all of borrowers' debts, and failed to properly verify sources of funds.[6]

Toxic mortgages were not the only thing poisoning Patricia's neighborhood. Several miles away are the Stringfellow Acid Pits, a site so contaminated by hazardous waste that the Environmental Protection Agency (EPA) declared that it poses a risk to human health and the environment. Beginning in 1956, major corporations dumped 34 million gallons of industrial waste into an unlined evaporation pond at the site. The contaminants, which came from producing metal finishing, electroplating, and DDT, migrated into the underlying, highly permeable soils and then into the groundwater table, resulting in a contaminated plume extending two miles downstream. The EPA has cited seven additional polluters in the neighborhood. Stringfellow has affected the local drinking water supply and negatively impacted home values.[7]

Much as she preferred her new home to living in Watts or West LA, Patricia had bought into a new development at the worst possible time. The house for which she paid $386,000 in 2006, with a huge down payment, was valued at a little over $300,000 by late 2014. Due to a combination of bad timing and fraudulent mortgage products, many on her block and in her neighborhood had lost their homes and, with them, all of their wealth. Patricia still had her home, but when we talked in 2010, she had lost the $112,000 down payment and all her equity. She lamented, "Now, there's nothing there. All the equity is gone, and I still owe more than the house is worth." When Patricia applied to modify her loan, she told the loan modification program officer that she "was burned . . . bit by a shark." Angry at being a casualty of the real estate market, she declared that she wished she had kept her money under a cushion. Home ownership was meant to provide for her retirement and to help her two daughters pay for college. In 2010, her retirement plan was in jeopardy, and her daughters needed scholarships and loans to continue their educations.

When I returned to Patricia's neighborhood in early 2015, things were looking better. There were no "for sale" signs, the houses looked to be in good repair, and all of the lawns were spruced up. One might never guess that the subdivision had been ravaged by the foreclosure crisis and witnessed a tremendous stripping of housing wealth. The market had culled those who could not keep up with their mortgages, who lost jobs, or who were working at lower salaries. The fortunes of families and communities can change quickly, and seeing clearly the challenges people face and how they adapt to them requires following their trajectories over a period. Today, Patricia is meeting the challenges thrown her way. Without marrying a millionaire, she has recovered from credit card debt and aims to be debt-free. Her house's value is stabilizing, even rising, while her modified mortgage is affordable, reducing her monthly payments by $500. She has a savings goal of "at least $10,000 a year," she tells me. "Put it like that." Accompanying her new economic stability is a perceptible sense of optimism in her attitude. Today, she feels secure, "really fortunate and blessed." To Patricia, the future looks bright.

Patricia Arrora's story is indicative of the crucial factors shaping the ups and downs of American family life and economic mobility today. With hard work and home ownership she gained dignity, respect, and upward mobility. She overcame recession and foreclosure challenges that often result in downward mobility. Most importantly, she faced and triumphed over challenges that made her path harder than it ought to have been: race and lack of wealth.

IN RECENT YEARS, AS LIVING STANDARDS FOR MANY FAMILIES have declined and productivity, income, and wealth gains have flowed to the very top, a new conversation about inequality has emerged in the United States. The Occupy Wall Street movement, which began in the fall of 2011, splashed inequality across the front pages and provided space for discussions about historically high income and wealth disparities and their causes. The movement pitted the wealthiest and most powerful 1 percent against 99 percent of Americans. Thomas Piketty's best-selling 2014 book, *Capital in the Twenty-First Century*, brought attention to a different kind of inequality with a focus on capital. Yet many popular and academic accounts of inequality, spurred by media coverage and the emerging national discourse, continued to focus on income disparities, economic class, and the mega-rich. A preoccupation with income led to an insufficient understanding of the new inequality that left wealth out of the picture. President Barack Obama provided perhaps the crowning moment in this new public attention to economic inequality when he proclaimed in a December 2014 speech that inequality "is the defining challenge of our time."[8] But the president's speech referenced income inequality eleven times and wealth inequality once. Leaving wealth out of the conversation is a crucial mistake, giving fodder to those who would make personal poverty the result of personal failings.

Wealth inequality in the United States is uncommonly high. The wealthiest 1 percent owned 42 percent of all wealth in 2012 and took in 18 percent of all income. Each year the Allianz Group, the world's largest financial service company, calculates each country's Gini coefficient—a measure of inequality in which zero indicates perfect equality and one hundred perfect inequality, or one person owning all the wealth. In 2015, the United States had the highest wealth inequality among industrialized nations, with a score of 80.56.[9] Allianz dubbed the USA the "Unequal States of America."

Wealth concentration has followed a U-shaped pattern over the last hundred years. It was high in the beginning of the twentieth century, with wealth inequality reaching its previous peak during the Depression, in 1929. It fell from 1929 to 1978 and has continuously increased since then. By 2012, the share of wealth owned by the top 0.1 percent was three times higher than in the late 1970s, growing from 7 percent in 1979 to 22 percent in 2012. The bottom 90 percent's wealth share has steadily declined since the mid-1980s.[10]

The rise of wealth inequality is almost entirely due to the increase in the top 0.1 percent's wealth share. The steady decline in the bottom 90 percent's wealth share has struck middle-class families in particular. Half the population has less than $500 in savings. In our interviews we heard the concerns of those who had more month than paycheck.[11]

Wealth is not just a matter of money. As our interviews revealed, wealth is also about power, status, opportunity, identity, and self-image. Wealth confers transformative advantages, while lack of it brings tremendous disadvantages. A family's income reflects educational and occupational achievements, but wealth is needed to solidify these achievements to build a solid foundation of economic security. Wealth is a fundamental pillar of economic security, and without it, as many of the families we interviewed experienced firsthand, hard-won gains are easily lost.

The explanations for economic inequality are many. One prominent line holds that individual values and characteristics either promote or hinder achievement and prosperity. Inequality, in this view, results from poor people's laziness and lack of work ethic, the decline of traditional marriage, an influx of unskilled, uneducated immigrants, and dependence on welfare. Our interviews contradict such arguments—the people we spoke with, rich and poor, had broadly similar values and aspirations—and reveal instead the importance of policy and institutional factors. Other theories focus on such factors as market forces in a globalizing economy, technological change, policies, and politics.[12]

This book takes a different tack, arguing that we must understand wealth and income inequality together with racial inequality. Despite recent attention to racial disparities in policing, mass deportation, persistent residential segregation, attacks on voting rights, and other manifestations of racial injustice, the conversation about widening economic inequality largely leaves out race, as if that gap's causes, its harshest consequences, and its potential solutions are race neutral. Whether they focus on the widening gulf between the very top and various segments further down the distribution ladder, on the fortunes of the bottom 40 percent, on the dwindling of the middle class, or simply on the growing share garnered by the best-off, traditional accounts emphasize class and economics as the central (and sometimes only) explanation. As a result, much of our national discourse about inequality sees disparities as universals that impact all groups in the same ways, and many of the policy ideas proposed to address it fail to recognize the racially disparate distributional impact of universal-sounding solutions.[13] Recent movements such as the Color of Change, the Dreamers, and Black Lives Matter are vigorously trying to recenter the inequality conversation to include race, ethnicity, and immigration. I have been inspired and heartened by the new public conversation about inequality. At the same time, I am frustrated that once again it looks like attention to class is trumping a reckoning with race.

For it is crucial to understand that the trends toward greater income and wealth inequality are converging with a widening racial wealth gap. The typical African American family today has less than a dime of wealth for every dollar of wealth owned by a typical white family. The civil rights movement and the landmark legislation of the 1960s helped to open educational and professional opportunities and to produce an African American middle class. But despite these hard-won advances, as a study following the same set of families for twenty-nine years shows, the gap between white and black family wealth has widened at an alarming pace, increasing nearly threefold over the past generation (see Figure 1.1). Looking at a representative sample of Americans in 2013, the median net wealth of white families was $142,000, compared to $11,000 for African American families and $13,700 for Hispanic families. This racial wealth gap means that even black families with incomes comparable to those of white families have much less wealth to use to cushion unemployment or a personal crisis, to apply as a down payment on a home, to secure a place for their families in a strong, resource-rich neighborhood, to send their children to private schools, to start a business, or to plan for retirement.

In short, the basic pillars of economic security—wealth and income—are today distributed vastly inequitably along racial and ethnic lines. African Americans' historical disadvantage has become baked into the American economy. African Americans are effectively stymied from generating and retaining wealth of their own not simply by continuing racial discrimination but also by senseless policies that protect existing wealth—wealth that often originated at times of even more intense racial discrimination, if not specifically from racial plunder. Race and wealth have intertwined throughout our nation's history. Too often missing in today's dialogue about inequality is this binding race and wealth linkage. Failure to tackle the nexus of race and wealth will lead, at best, to only small ameliorations at the worst edges of inequality.

Figure 1.1 Median Net Wealth by Race, 1984–2013

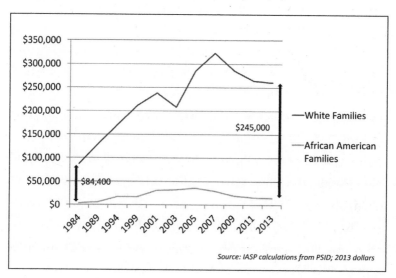

Source: IASP calculations from PSID; 2013 dollars

Major demographic shifts that are increasingly diversifying America and threatening to sharpen racial and ethnic fault lines further exacerbate the dangers of historically high wealth and income inequality and a widening racial wealth gap. America is becoming a majority-minority nation. Newborns of color outnumbered white newborns for the first time in 2013. America's population growth stems from higher birth rates among families of color and from immigration, especially among Asians and Latinos, while its white population is aging. In 2014, only 21 percent of seniors, but 47 percent of youth, were nonwhite. Demographics are not destiny; yet our institutions, from schools to the workforce to communities to government, are just beginning to confront challenges of racial diversity they were not designed to face, are ill prepared to meet, and often resist.

Our institutions grew out of an assumed everlasting, politically dominant white majority. The nation has not yet imagined who we are together.

The phrase "toxic inequality" describes a powerful and unprecedented convergence: historic and rising levels of wealth and income inequality in an era of stalled mobility, intersecting with a widening racial wealth gap, all against the backdrop of changing racial and ethnic demographics.

I call this kind of inequality toxic because, over time and generations, it builds upon itself. Wealth and race map together to consolidate historic injustices, which now weave through neighborhoods and housing markets, educational institutions, and labor markets, creating an increasingly divided opportunity structure. So long as we have entrenched wealth inequality intertwined with racial inequality, we cannot even begin to bend the arc toward equity.

Toxic inequality is also noxious in that it makes these challenges harder to tackle. High levels of material inequality are inherently destabilizing, heightening social tensions. Janet Yellen, chair of the board of governors of the Federal Reserve System, has warned that economic inequality "can shape [and] determine the ability of different groups to participate equally in a democracy and have grave effects on social stability over time."[14] Thomas Piketty argues that extremely high levels of wealth inequality are "incompatible with the meritocratic values and principles of social justice fundamental to modern democratic societies" and warns that a drift toward oligarchy is a real danger.[15] The new inequality is especially politically poisonous because most people of all races feel stuck in place, finding it harder to believe that hard work, sacrifice, and innovation are going to pay off and lead to a better life. People are apt to look for someone to blame, and America's changing demographics encourage racial division, resentment of other groups, and prejudice. These forces have complicated economic policymaking throughout our history, but they are especially dangerous today, given the urgent need to address the particular economic disadvantages facing people of color.

We are just beginning to understand one further dimension of toxic inequality: a phenomenon we might call "toxic inequality syndrome." Are there emotional and even physiological consequences for families and individuals exposed to repeated, persistent economic trauma, frustrated ambitions, and cumulative downward spirals? We know that there is a strong relationship between adversity and social outcomes throughout the life course, with greater frequency of adverse events leading to worse outcomes.[16] One adverse event increases the likelihood of a cascade of other stressful and traumatic events. Research has documented the negative impact of a wide variety of stress-inducing events, including community violence, accidents, life-threatening illnesses, loss of economic status, and incidences of racism. We also know that financial resources shield families from economic and social trauma, lessen the impact of some trauma, enable more rapid recovery, and reduce the risk of subsequent adverse events.[17] Yet many of the families we spoke to experienced multiple forms of adversity—foreclosure, violence, unsafe neighborhoods, incarceration, disability, sudden or chronic family illness, family breakup, unemployment or loss of wages, declining living standards—without adequate wealth resources and without the sorts of family, institutional, community, or policy support that can also foster family resiliency. In the stories in subsequent chapters, we will encounter amazing resiliency, and we also will meet families who became overwhelmed by the stress and trauma associated with toxic inequality.

America's response to toxic inequality will set our future course for generations. The current magnitude of inequality robs the nation of human potential and promise, sapping aspirations and distorting futures. Earned achievements have become uncoupled from financial rewards and personal well-being. Frustrated ambitions and stalled social mobility foment racial anxieties. Without bold changes, we will keep heading toward greater inequality and become even more polarized along class and racial lines. The tiny segments of the population that are doing well will continue to do so, and the vast majority will try even harder just to stay in place. The rich and powerful will continue to write rules that protect and expand their vast advantages at the expense of those struggling to keep pace, especially younger adults and families and communities of color. As differences magnify, those groups facing the brunt of inequality, stalled mobility, and lost status will more critically interrogate the legitimacy of governmental and economic systems. Such an interrogation of deep structures is necessary and productive as long as it uncovers drivers of inequality. However, an explanation that does nothing more than pander to racial, ethnic, and class fears will short-circuit solutions. To avoid this bleak future and bend current trends in the direction of shared prosperity, we must transform the deep structures that foster inequality.

Policy solutions must be bold, transformative, and at a scale sufficient to reach the families and communities most affected by toxic inequality.

THIS BOOK PLACES OUR FAMILY INTERVIEWS FRONT AND center in building a comprehensive understanding of what toxic inequality is and why it matters so much, and it proposes proven, evidence-informed policy solutions that can equitably increase prosperity for American families. Patricia Arrora's story captures the major themes of well-being, opportunity, and inequality in the United States. Wealth, or its absence, begins where we begin: in the neighborhood where we are born. Work helps us improve our earning power and shapes our adult lives. In time, if we're born to the right family in the right neighborhood, if we secure the right job, and if the policy landscape favors it, we might amass a certain amount of wealth. At the end of the day, we might pass that wealth to the next generation in the form of inheritance. And through it all, government policies can either help multiply our opportunities and our wealth or obliterate them. Patricia's story turns on these key factors: wealth and financial resources; community, home, and family; work; inheritance and kin networks; and the opportunities and challenges posed by government policy. This book's organization reflects those themes, drawing throughout on our team's interviews with families in 1998 and 1999 and from 2010 to 2012, supplemented by nationally representative data, in the hopes of illuminating how these factors work together to shape a family's well-being.

The first chapter looks squarely at how families accumulate wealth, not primarily as an end in itself but as a tool to stave off crises and create advantages and opportunities for mobility. It also examines how the absence of wealth turns small crises into major disasters, severely narrows opportunities, and inhibits mobility. The stories of the Breslin and Johnson families make these dynamics clear. They also reveal the importance of kin and family networks. Successful families of color are more likely than middle-class white families to need to help out relatives or friends in times of need, and when they do so, they have fewer resources left over to move ahead themselves.

Our examination then moves in Chapter 2 to homes and communities, the largest reservoirs of wealth and opportunity for the vast majority of families. Chapter 2 explores the story of the Andrews family, whose challenges and decisions highlight the enduring significance of race and economics in home values and the advantages and disadvantages of neighborhoods and location. The stories of three other families in this chapter further illustrate how neighborhood inequality powerfully shapes the overall contours of toxic inequality.

The book then turns from home to work. Chapter 3 introduces the Ackermans, whose story affords us a broader understanding of how jobs, income, and benefits drive opportunity and inequality. Earnings convert to wealth differently according to a job's benefit structure. Access to the kinds of workplace benefits that result in wealth accumulation and greater mobility varies according to work sector and is thus shaped by occupational segregation. Other family interviews illustrate how minority workers' income is comparatively isolated from wealth-growing mechanisms. Pay stubs approaching parity hide systematic discrimination that drives both the wealth gap and the widening racial wealth gap.

Some fortunate families have wonderful head starts in life, with wealth facilitating multiple chances to succeed even in the face of challenges. Chapter 4 examines the important matter of inheritance. We meet the Clarks, whose inherited wealth permits a kind of life well beyond the means of their earned income. Their children attend strong, resource-rich private schools and grow up in an upscale neighborhood. A look at other families illustrates the kinds of benefits that smaller inheritance and transfers transmit. Those without such transfers suffer as a result.

In all of these realms, government policy functions to increase inequality. In theory, the goal of social policy is to widen opportunities, minimize barriers to success, promote well-being, and help build equity into prosperity. But Chapter 5 demonstrates that the distributional effect of core government policies is actually to create, maintain, and widen inequality.

Our exploration of toxic inequality concludes with a look back at the families we have met throughout the book, interrogating how it might be in our power, as a country, to change their lives for the better. A mobility policy agenda would include family wealth-building policies such as children's savings accounts, an expanded Family Self-Sufficiency program, housing mobility and stability measures, and policies concerning better wages and benefits and family supports. An equity agenda would reform existing policies that deepen inequality, such as the tax code's treatment of mortgage interest, retirement contributions, and inheritance. The book's policy recommendations offer a path toward changing the lives of the families our team met and stemming the tide of toxic inequality for all.

Patricia Arrora is one of the nearly two hundred individuals or couples who shared their dreams and disappointments, joys and sorrows. One life story cannot capture the complexity and individuality of American families and their struggle for a better life, but Patricia's story and others collectively help to reveal how toxic inequality stymies family, community, and economic well-being. This is why real people's lives are at the core of this book. Far too often, toxic inequality has kept them from achieving the full scope of their dreams for themselves and their children. The first step toward making change is to tell their stories and understand how their individual challenges connect to the powerful forces that have brought us all to this moment of crisis.

$$= 1 =$$

WEALTH MATTERS

TRULY UNDERSTANDING THE DEVASTATING EFFECTS OF WEALTH inequality requires a clear sense of how and why wealth itself matters in the lives of real families, how they acquire it, and what they use it for. Whether earned or inherited, wealth provides life-changing opportunities, advantages, and protections for some, while its lack poses constant, challenging barriers difficult to overcome through hard work or doing the right thing, like saving for a child's education.

Inequality means one thing if it describes the difference between poverty and middle-class status or the affluent and the superrich. No doubt, it's a useful term for sketching the difference between a well-paid lawyer or a hedge fund manager and those who are barely scraping by. Our thinking about inequality is regularly a snapshot of a given moment. Yet thinking about differences in inequality's trajectories over time is crucial to understanding its impact on families and society. In some societies, members of succeeding generations have roughly equal chances of moving ahead or falling back based on their own accomplishments. When this is not the case, as in the United States, the spin of the birth lottery becomes a dominant factor in a family's wealth trajectory. Inequality becomes a central determinant of one's future. This brings the importance of wealth to center stage—how having it helps, how not having it hinders.

Overall the empirical evidence in the United States and elsewhere is compelling and suggests long-lasting advantages for children of wealthier families and for families who have acquired their own financial assets.[1] For example, a child born into a wealthy family is more than six times as likely to become a wealthy adult than a child born into a poor family.[2] Researchers have pinpointed strong relationships between family wealth and children's educational outcomes, which connect to lifetime earnings from employment; children from the highest-income families were eight times more likely than children from low-income families to obtain a bachelor's degree by age twenty-four.[3] One might expect these advantages to show up in economic security, but they also include robust wealth effects for health and psychological well-being. One landmark British survey identifies wealth as a bigger influence than jobs or educational achievement in determining the life span of people age fifty or older. A quarter of the men in the lowest wealth quintile had died within a six-year period, compared to one in ten of those in the highest quintile.[4] Wealth, often entwining with race, can affect a family's health status through disparate coverage, care quality, and copayment levels. More than two in five blacks (39 percent) and 42 percent of Hispanics said they did not get some form of needed medical care in the past year because they could not afford it.[5] Wealth provides a lifetime of financial, health, and other advantages.[6]

All this suggests the important role wealth plays within families across generations. Wealth operates over time as a source of opportunities and a safety net for families, while a lack of it holds families back. This chapter shows how institutional factors account for wealth movement both over a working lifetime and across generations for families in the first decade of the twenty-first century; it examines what distinguishes wealth gainers from those merely holding ground or falling behind, and it indicates how the weaving of race into the institutional fabric has become more apparent and concrete. This chapter contends that the wealth inequality and racial wealth gap puzzles are actually one and the same, with wealth and racial inequality inextricably linked, as they have been throughout our history. Given the large racial wealth gap and the importance of wealth, we need to see clearly how wealth works for families—as we will in this chapter with two black families. This journey begins with a Boston parent named Cindy Breslin.

CINDY BRESLIN'S ELEVEN-YEAR-OLD SON WANTED TO BE A lawyer or fireman, and her five-year-old daughter wanted to be a nurse or a doctor. Keneysha played with a toy doctor's kit all the time, even promising her mother that she was going to take care of her when Cindy grew older. But the leap from playing doctor to attending medical school is a big one for practically anybody, especially for someone growing up in poverty, as Keneysha was. As it would turn out, despite Cindy's aspirations for her daughter, Keneysha's dream was beyond her reach. Her older brother would find low-wage work.

I first met Cindy, a thirty-two-year-old African American single mother, in 1998. We talked at her rent-subsidized apartment in the hardscrabble Boston neighborhood of Charlestown, famous from movies like *The Town*. A learning disability made it very difficult for Cindy to participate fully in the paid economy. Work at odd maintenance jobs where she lived, plus a rental subsidy, food stamps, and disability benefits, brought her income to $18,600. Cindy exemplifies how current welfare policy in the United States temporarily assists family survival but does not facilitate advancement. In the small kitchen, as Keneysha played with her doctor's kit, Cindy described how her income was not sufficient to provide any security or enable her to get ahead. She was one of 34.5 million people, or 12.7 percent of the population, officially living in poverty in 1998.

But those hardships did not dampen Cindy's dreams for Keneysha. She was putting money away every month for her daughter's college education; against steep odds, and contrary to the granite-hard assumptions of experts and pundits that poor people cannot save, she had already set aside $1,000. Cindy also had a refreshing hostility toward credit cards, saying she did not have any and never would because she did not like to owe anybody money. It is worth noting that today in half of the states, though not in Massachusetts, the act of saving for a child's education is held against parents like Cindy, counting against and even jeopardizing their social assistance eligibility. Families struggling with poverty are discouraged, even penalized, for investing and saving to give their kids a brighter future. For well-off families, the same act is a marker of good parenting, even incentivized by our tax system. Some families are rewarded while others are punished for saving for a child's higher education.

Cindy envisioned Keneysha on a green college campus, with grass, trees, quiet spaces, quadrangles, brick buildings, and safety, very much the opposite of her dense, urban Charlestown neighborhood. Cindy kept using the word "safe" to describe her vision of her daughter's future—a stark contrast to her everyday reality of crime and frequent threats to physical safety.

Twelve years later, much had changed for Cindy and Keneysha. Now living in the Dorchester section of Boston, the two were not doing as well as before. Keneysha's twenty-three-year-old brother had moved out and was working full-time at a low-wage job. Making ends meet was getting harder and harder. Cindy's income was $19,600, just $1,000 more than in 1998. But her living expenses—rent, food, utilities, clothing, and the needs of a growing teenage daughter—kept rising year by year. "It just seems like everything is going up," she said. "Rent is a little bit higher . . . high gas bills . . . high light bills . . . high telephone bill, and even the food is kind of high." To maintain her 1998 standard of living, she would have needed close to $25,000 in 2010. The nearly $6,000 shortfall meant her living standard had declined by 28 percent since our first conversation. Welfare policy changes negatively affected her income, driving her into deeper poverty. Her rental assistance did not keep pace with inflation, disability allotments did not include adequate cost-of-living adjustments, and other assistance was phased out. Formally Cindy's income hovered around the official poverty line, but the family's declining living standard spoke a greater truth: for Cindy and her kids, the month lasted longer than their resources.

Living standards were also declining for people other than those relying on social assistance. Cindy's downward income experience matched that of most Americans: the real median family income in 2010 was 2.7 percent lower than in 2007, adjusted for inflation.

Like other families with low, stagnant, or declining incomes, Cindy sought ways to cope. She tried to save on food, for instance. "I'll make a chicken casserole, or I'll make a big, big pot of spaghetti, or I'll make a beef stew," she said, describing meals that would last for "a couple of days that we can stretch through." Still, by the last week of the month, Cindy said, "I usually struggle. I usually run out of most of the stuff I need, like bread, ketchup, meat. I usually have to eat noodles, sandwiches, or maybe just noodles." With little income and facing ever-rising expenses, everyday life for Cindy was full of hard choices and sacrifices.

But the declining fortunes of Cindy and her family in 2010 also resulted from her lack of financial assets—her lack of wealth. Income and financial assets are both crucial to a family's well-being and capacity to absorb setbacks and move forward. Managing personal crises or economic events like the Great Recession is all the more difficult without the safety net that wealth can provide. Cindy's savings of $1,000 in 1998—remarkable as they were, given her situation—left her far below the asset poverty threshold, which was then $3,413 for her family. In this, she was not alone. Research shows that 44 percent of families fall below the asset poverty line, leaving them less ready to meet an emergency or get through tough times.[7] Absent a rainy-day fund or emergency resources to weather a financial storm, such families are liable to fall back on credit cards or other stopgap measures that only make it more difficult to clamber out of poverty.

This was certainly true of Cindy Breslin. Although twelve years earlier she had vowed not to owe anybody anything, in 2010 she owed $1,200 on two credit cards with exorbitant rates. Her monthly payments only covered the interest charges and did not dent the balance. The $1,000 she had stowed away in a kindergarten-to-college savings plan for Keneysha had dwindled to $30. She had paid funeral expenses for her fiancé, a Vietnam War veteran, which the Veterans Administration (VA) would not fully cover. A stroke of bad luck made things worse. A car accident left Keneysha in rehabilitation and lots of pain, and out of school, for nearly a year. Cindy paid for out-of-pocket medical expenses from her meager savings and then resorted to credit cards. Her daughter, who had dreamed as a five-year-old of attending college and becoming a doctor, now hoped to finish high school and eventually find work as a nurse's aide.

The public discourse, media, and policy often depict families like Cindy's—surviving as best they can on public assistance—as the undeserving poor, the product of a dependency culture and perverse incentives that reduce social assistance as income from work increases, lacking personal responsibility. People like Cindy, who scrape by on public assistance, become the objects of derision in the media and victim-blaming ridicule in the public arena. These sorts of derogating depictions have bulwarked efforts to reduce public assistance for poor or struggling families in the last two decades. That narrative blinds us to the real lives and choices of people and families struggling with poverty. For instance, it conveniently skims over how Cindy spent most of her savings to bury the man she was about to marry, a war veteran whose army benefits did not cover a proper funeral.

With the clarity of hindsight, Cindy, like anyone else, regretted some of her decisions. Before our first interview in 1998, she had received a legal settlement for a hate crime when living in public housing, which she used to support her aging and ill mother, place a deposit on a new apartment, fund an excursion to Toys "R" Us, and purchase clothes and trips for her children—things she felt her poverty had denied them. Years later, she lamented that maybe she could have spent that money more productively. But the government policies and economic structures she confronted constrained her decisions. Cindy's private resources compensated for inadequate public policy concerning long-term care for the elderly. Cindy and Keneysha Breslin deserved better options that would have allowed them to build the wealth needed to work through financial crises and achieve their dreams.

In America, wealth is a necessary foundation for building a better life. In Cindy's family, an absence of wealth had dire consequences, holding her and her children back, forcing them to run hard just to stay in place. Their lack of assets during Keneysha's childhood means, furthermore, that she will likely lack wealth as an adult as well, holding back another generation.

While most families use income to meet daily expenses, wealth provides a store of financial resources that families utilize to get through income-reducing negative life events like medical emergencies, family crises, or personal troubles.[8] Beyond providing a safety net, wealth also allows people to improve their education and skills, buy a home, invest, start a business, and help other family members through tough times or to get ahead. Yet access to the kind of wealth that allows one to make a down payment on a modest home, attend two years at a community college, or start a business—about $14,000—is vastly unequal.[9] Less than half (46 percent) of all US families and only about one in five African American and Latino families have adequate financial wealth for these kinds of mobility opportunities. Policies in the past and present have enabled wide-open opportunities for some and kept them from others. The top 1 percent of US households controls 42 percent of the nation's wealth, and nearly half of the wealth accumulated over the past thirty years has gone to the top 0.1 percent of households.[10] The portion of wealth held by the bottom 90 percent of Americans continues to shrink.[11] Wealth disparities are even larger across distributions by race. The typical black family holds between five and ten cents for each dollar held by a white family. In 2013, the average white family owned $13 for every $1 owned by a typical black family and $10 for every $1 owned by the average Latino family.[12] And there is clear evidence that wealth inequality between whites and families of color is growing.[13]

Wealth inequality impacts more than those we think of as poor, like Cindy Breslin and her family. As we have seen, wealth is critical to coping with emergencies and taking advantage of mobility opportunities. The limits imposed by a lack of wealth hold not just for poor families like Cindy's but generally for middle-class families as well. And poor and middle-class black families confront extra hurdles in gaining and keeping wealth. The Johnson family illustrates some of the ways that wealth, or the lack thereof, impacts black middle-class families.

Michelle Johnson was a child, just eleven years old and living in segregated southern Florida, when Martin Luther King Jr. addressed a tense nation in 1963 at the March on Washington for Jobs and Freedom. That year, African American home ownership stood at 38.1 percent, 26.2 percent lower than the rate for white families. Black Americans were four times as likely to live below the poverty line and 2.2 times more likely to be unemployed; median family income was 60.5 percent of that of white families; and 27 percent of blacks held high school degrees versus 51 percent of whites. Barriers to black home ownership included economic inequality and a slew of government policies that systematically locked African Americans out. The United States did not yet have a fair housing or fair lending law. Residential segregation was the taken-for-granted norm. Redlining, whereby banks and insurance companies refuse or limit loans, mortgages, and insurance policies within specific geographic areas, especially minority or highly diverse neighborhoods—a practice originated by the Federal Housing Administration (FHA)—was still rampant. Home mortgages financed by the FHA and the

VA—the largest government-backed property-owning and wealth-generating opportunities since the Homestead Acts of the nineteenth century—largely excluded African Americans. Federal investments in transportation infrastructure also encouraged segregated suburban residential developments. This cluster of policies created vast wealth-building opportunities for whites while tethering blacks to segregated, lower-resourced, inner-city neighborhoods.

Michelle's mother and father both worked for an insurance company, and neither had a college education. When we interviewed her in 1998, Michelle bitterly remembered growing up in segregated Florida, living in a black neighborhood across the tracks from an affluent white neighborhood she didn't dare visit. She was one of the first African Americans in her junior high school. Her high school memories include being chased home from school by some white boys and thinking she was ugly because no one wanted to date a black girl. She decided not to run for class president or prom queen because she was one of only a few black students. She chose to attend a historically black college, looking to have an experience where she was not part of a tiny minority.

In 1974, Michelle graduated with a degree in history, along with nearly $10,000 in student loan debt. She began teaching junior high school in Florida, where she met her husband, Kendrick. In the 1980s, Kendrick was offered an exciting high-profile opportunity in Los Angeles's booming news broadcasting industry, and with their two young daughters, the family moved west. It was hard for Michelle to find a teaching job, so she reluctantly stayed at home to take care of her two children. She was substitute-teaching while looking for a full-time teaching job when we first met her in 1998.

By 2010, Kendrick's pay had climbed to a robust $110,000. As a married, college-educated, professional couple with a six-figure family income, the Johnsons were very much members of a new African American middle class. But they struggled to convert Kendrick's income into economic security or wealth. His high-paying job was unsteady, lacking key health-care or pension benefits that would help the couple defray medical expenses associated with their seventeen-year-old daughter Desi's neuropsychiatric disorder, diagnosed as Tourette's syndrome, or build wealth. Desi's older sister had graduated college the year before, and that, too, had commanded family resources. Because of their success they often helped out less fortunate family members, particularly their aging parents, who had had only limited opportunities to build wealth themselves. Kendrick reflected, "It's really odd. . . . [W]hat's really bizarre is people think you make all this money. When you have aging parents who you're helping and you've got a daughter who's going through what she's going through and another daughter in college, it just gets spread out so thin."

In 2004, Kendrick was laid off. He and Michelle cashed out $18,000 in savings and retirement accounts to cover living expenses for the eight months he was out of work. Kendrick eventually found a new job on the East Coast, 3,000 miles away. The long unemployment spell and relocation expenses took a huge toll on the family's financial assets; they also created personal stress and strained the couple's marriage. In 2006, Michelle moved back to her family homestead in

Florida with their two daughters, while Kendrick worked in New Jersey trying to stabilize the family's financial situation. Most of his income went to supporting the family and paying off debts incurred from Desi's medical condition. Kendrick told us how he lived out of his car for two years and showered at hotels. Michelle was still unable to reenter the paid workforce, as Desi was being bullied at school and the local school system in Florida did not have the resources, expertise, or inclination to meet her special education needs. Michelle and Kendrick decided homeschooling was the best solution, sacrificing the additional income that Michelle might have earned if she had worked for pay instead.

Despite these challenges, by 2012 the Johnsons were slowly recovering financially. Michelle had found some part-time work, and together they were making about $120,000. But the geographic separation and financial stress took an even greater toll, as Kendrick considered the marriage over, though Michelle did not. Kendrick had started a media business and managed to save $32,000 in a retirement account. He hoped the money would grow and provide retirement security for both him and Michelle. He promised to "see both of us through retirement, whether we're together or not. . . . I'm just not the disappearing black guy, you know? I just am not going to be that. . . . I'm going to supply." Michelle, meanwhile, reflected on the advice her mother had given her thirty years earlier: "I'm sending you to college so that you can always be able to take care of yourself. You won't have to depend on anyone to take care of you." Now, Michelle found herself in "a pretty bad situation." I asked her if she would have done anything differently, knowing how things had turned out. Although she had needed to care for a child with disabilities, she regretted that she had not worked consistently or developed a career of her own. She found herself at fifty-eight years old "in Florida and my husband is in New Jersey saying that we are split up and we aren't married anymore, blah, blah, blah." Michelle returned to her mother's wisdom once again: "But I did know it was going to turn out like this, didn't I? Because my mother told me."

Michelle had traveled a great distance from her segregated upbringing and menacing high school experiences. But as she and her family negotiated the peaks and valleys of life, they faced major barriers that many white families do not. They confronted economic challenges with only the small safety net of their limited personal wealth, and they were responsible for taking care of an extended family that lacked similar assets. Michelle's story is one of successes based on merit and newly opened opportunities. But in a turn familiar to many American families, it is also a story of being knocked off track too easily due to lack of wealth. Unemployment, medical emergencies, disability, decimated savings, tuition costs, depleted retirement accounts, a job far from home, homeschooling out of necessity, family stress, and separation—all have held her and her family back and derailed their dreams.

Conservative politicians and policymakers and some liberals often propose wedlock as a pathway out of poverty and a route to mobility and well-being. Democratic and Republican senators (Ben Cardin and Mike DeWine) and congressmen sponsored President George W. Bush's 2002 Building Strong Families Program. Promotion of matrimony and marriage counseling over more than a decade has been costly; yet rigorous evaluation studies have shown no effective results of promoting marriage, saving marriages, lowering out-of-wedlock births, or reducing poverty.[14] Nonetheless, marriage as a silver-bullet solution to poverty remains a deep-rooted meme and political mainstay. For instance, Senator Marco Rubio has declared, "The truth is, the greatest tool to lift children and families from poverty is one that decreases the probability of child poverty. . . . But it isn't a government spending program. It's called marriage."[15] It is true that single-parent families are more likely to fall below the income and asset poverty lines than two-parent families. But this is a function not of marriage itself but of the increased likelihood of two incomes. More adult earners mean more income, less spending on child care, and less poverty. If anything, as the Johnson family's story suggests, the marriage-cures-poverty narrative is backward. Poverty, highly volatile family incomes, and unsteady paid employment are barriers to lasting and successful marriages. The growth of single-mother households has contributed much less to increasing poverty, particularly in recent years, than has rising income inequality. Between 1979 and 2013, increased poverty rates accounted for mounting income inequality four times greater than changes in family structure; elevated poverty increased it 7.1 percent versus 1.6 percent for changes in family structure.[16] As in the Johnsons' case, removal of anchors of stability can set in motion a cascade of other stressful and traumatic events. Kendrick's losing his job unleashed economic, psychological, family, and marital stresses from which he and Michelle could not recover.

For the Johnsons, life during the decade that included the Great Recession was, despite their constant striving, a time of advancing while simultaneously falling behind. Although the civil rights movement may have succeeded in removing legal and social barriers to full citizenship for all African Americans and produced tremendous gains in education, employment, and wealth accumulation for some African Americans, much of its economic and social justice agenda remains unfinished. And when it comes to wealth, the Great Recession wiped out many of the gains, producing the largest loss of minority wealth in US history. A Pew report put the wealth loss at over 50 percent for African Americans and at 66 percent for the Hispanic community.[17]

THE BRESLINS AND THE JOHNSONS DEMONSTRATE HOW FAMI-lies build wealth and the challenges they face in doing so, especially among African Americans. Of course theirs are but two stories that illustrate key dynamics connecting wealth accumulation—or the lack thereof—to family opportunities, mobility, and well-being. A more systematic discussion will highlight factors shaping how families gain or lose wealth—that is, the role of institutions/structures like home ownership and markets, race, and good or bad fortune, rather than personal virtue or decision making. Comprehensive national surveys reveal that those able to increase their wealth generally enjoy increasing family incomes, consistent long-term home ownership, occupational advancement in some cases, and larger quantities of family financial assistance, including through inheritance.[18] In contrast, experiencing negative

personal, medical, and family events, living in poor neighborhoods, and being of color constrict a family's ability to
build and grow wealth. Before digging into these key drivers
in greater detail, it is worth noting that they reveal a striking
pattern connecting wealth acquisition to primarily institutional arenas like home ownership and occupation and family
and inheritance. Policy and institutions play a fundamental
role in building wealth over the life course and improving
well-being and opportunity.

By design, we interviewed parents of young children because this life phase is so crucial for family development.
Understanding wealth acquisition, utilization, and depletion
in families raising children is important for two critical reasons. First, parental wealth while children are growing up
foreshadows how well they will do in their adult lives.[19] The
parents' well-being and the child's future opportunities are
contingent on wealth accumulated during the child-rearing
years, which generally coincide with adults' high earning periods. Second, wealth accumulated by adults during these
years forms the foundation for what they will have to draw
upon later in their own lives, during retirement or when they
are less able to work to generate income.

A deeply held, popular ideal maintains that in America
a person can start with little, work hard, and become rich.[20]
Closely related is the belief that wealth rises and falls based
on hard work, personal character, and individual merit. Rigorous research on economic mobility tells a different story.
No matter how it is measured, economic mobility is far rarer
than assumed. For those at the top and the bottom of the
wealth distribution—the richest and the poorest people—it

is quite limited indeed.[21] Rises from poverty to affluence and falls from moneyed beginnings to straitened circumstances are statistical rarities. There are two main ways of measuring economic mobility. One can assess the amount of economic movement within the same generation over a family's working lifetime, usually referred to as intragenerational mobility. One can also examine economic mobility between generations—typically comparing parents and their adult children—which social scientists call intergenerational mobility. The value here is to evaluate how open or closed opportunities are today compared to yesterday and where we will be as a society tomorrow and to get a sense of how the United States compares to other societies. Knowing both how well families fare over a working lifetime and how well children do compared to their parents is important because that information gets to the heart of how well we are doing as a society and where we are headed.

Research on wealth mobility between generations shows some up and down movement, but moving up has become increasingly difficult. Envision the five wealth quintiles, each containing one-fifth of Americans sorted by wealth, as a wealth ladder with five rungs. A 2013 Pew study on wealth movement between generations found considerable wealth mobility as half of Americans had greater wealth holdings than their parents did at the same age, and 72 percent of adults situated in the bottom wealth quintile surpassed their parents' wealth. This would seem to suggest that things are getting better. With rising levels of overall wealth inequality, however, the rungs of the ladder are getting further apart, and it is becoming harder to move from one wealth quintile to another. Median wealth among those in the lowest quintile over the past generation has decreased by more than half compared to a generation ago, while at the top of the wealth distribution, median wealth has increased from just under $500,000 to almost $630,000 over the same period.[22] Families in the bottom and top quintiles alike tend to be stuck there,[23] and it is harder for a family to move up the ladder than it is to hold on to a position at the top.[24] Wealth has concentrated at the very top of the ladder,[25] a pattern reinforced by the inheritance of key financial resources, social networks, and cultural capital.[26]

Stickiness at the top and bottom of the wealth distribution ladder also pertains to family wealth mobility within one generation. For instance, 66 percent of those raised at the bottom of the wealth ladder remain on the bottom two rungs themselves, and 66 percent of those raised at the top of the wealth ladder remain on the top two rungs. Half of blacks (50 percent) raised at the bottom of the family wealth ladder remain stuck there as adults, compared with only a third (33 percent) of whites. More than two-thirds of blacks (68 percent) raised in the middle fall to the bottom two rungs of the ladder as adults compared with just under a third of whites (30 percent).[27] Only 23 percent of blacks raised in the middle surpass their parents' family wealth compared with over half (56 percent) of whites. African Americans tend to get blocked at the bottom, while whites at the top stay put.

Not only are black families much more likely to be stuck at the bottom of the income and wealth ladders, but between generations they also have a harder time moving ahead of their parents' family income and wealth than do whites.[28]

Whites are twice as likely as blacks to leave the bottom rung over a generation, and three out of four African Americans born to families in the bottom wealth quintile remain in the bottom half as adults. In contrast, whites born into the bottom quartile have almost even odds of ending up in the top half of the wealth distribution.[29] And African Americans are less likely to pass along earned status to the next generation: the adult children of most well-off African Americans are downwardly mobile in relation to their parents' wealth holdings.

The magnitude of wealth accumulated over the life course also differs by race. My team at the Institute on Assets and Social Policy (IASP) documented the differences in wealth (not including home equity) accumulated over a twenty-nine-year period by whites and by blacks.[30] The median white family started with $29,000 more in financial wealth in 1984 than the median black family but ended the study period in 2013 with $119,000 more (in dollars adjusted for inflation). In other words, white families accumulated wealth at three times the rate of black families. Similarly, an Urban Institute study found that white families in their thirties held three and a half times as much wealth as black families in the same age cohort in 1983.[31] By the time these same families were in their sixties in 2009, white families held seven times as much wealth.

The interviews we conducted with black and white parents in 1998 and 1999 and between 2010 and 2012 correspond with the results of the nationally representative surveys. Over the twelve-year period between interviews, the black families we interviewed gained significantly less wealth at the median than did the white families; they were far more likely to be stuck in lower wealth quintiles than were white families; and they experienced less upward mobility, especially into higher wealth quintiles. The ninety-seven families who gained wealth over the twelve years that separated our interviews did so because they owned homes in neighborhoods that allowed their home equity to rise, had good-paying jobs with robust benefits, and received financial assistance from extended family networks. Once again, institutional forces rather than individual behaviors drove wealth accumulation. Meanwhile, families experiencing wealth loss, stagnant wealth, or a consistent dearth of assets over the twelve-year period repeatedly talked about income-draining life events, such as unemployment, illness, onset of a disability, and loss of spouse through death, divorce, or separation. Various kinds of debt—including consumer debt and student loans—were major drags on family wealth. Those who lacked assets to draw upon during emergencies and unforeseen events tended to turn to debt to cover expenses, only to face credit terms that left them struggling to pay interest and barely touching the principal.

Place of residence was important to how much wealth a family managed to build and thus impacted mobility. Desirable, resource-rich neighborhoods allowed families to build housing wealth, which by far accounts for the largest wealth reservoir for middle- and lower-middle-class families. Two-thirds of net wealth held by the middle 60 percent of families is home equity. For families able to access home ownership in neighborhoods with higher-priced homes and stable values, building wealth in this way was a real possibility. But mere home ownership was not a magic bullet; purchasing a home in a neighborhood with low or volatile housing prices did not guarantee wealth. Race played a large role in which neighborhoods had stable and climbing versus volatile and declining housing values. Families were likelier to build wealth in predominantly white neighborhoods, especially high socioeconomic-status ones, while black and Latino neighborhoods more often saw greater home value volatility or declines. Other research has reinforced the importance of the neighborhood in the financial and social well-being of a family. Neighborhoods of residence impact intergenerational patterns of social, economic, and educational mobility.[32] Growing up in a low-income, racially segregated neighborhood reduces a child's ability to build financial security, gain an education, and accumulate assets over his or her lifetime.

Those families that increased their wealth between 1998 and 2010 had at least one earner with access to employment that provided wealth-building benefits such as matched defined contribution retirement accounts or traditional pensions (defined benefit plans), health insurance, education credits or investment, severance pay, and disability insurance. Some also enjoyed flexible work schedules that allowed them to accommodate the demands of child rearing and attend doctors' appointments and school meetings without taking time from paid work. Most wealth gainers had uninterrupted work histories, usually with the same employer. This kind of employment capital is key to building a wealth infrastructure.[33] In our interviews, black families experienced more disruptions in employment, and larger surveys confirm that African American workers continue to be concentrated in jobs that do not offer various wealth-building benefits.[34] For instance, while 65 percent of white workers had retirement plans in 2009, only 55.7 percent of black workers and 38 percent of Hispanic workers worked for employers offering such plans. Younger workers had the lowest percentage of retirement coverage by employer, reflecting both a changing economic structure and employers' lower tendency to offer plans to new workers.[35] These trends foreshadow a deeper discussion in a later chapter detailing the importance of occupations and work sectors to wealth escalators and the significant difference race makes in how wealth is institutionally structured.

The family interviews also revealed the importance of having an extended network of support from family and friends willing and able to share assets through gifts, inheritance, and direct payment of bills. Being part of a "web of wealth" was crucial to wealth mobility, lifting families beyond where their own earnings would otherwise place them.[36] Families with access to a well-resourced web of wealth were able to get help when they faced unemployment or some other loss of income. They also received help in paying for children's educational expenses, including private school and college tuition and fees for test prep programs and camps. In some cases, the web of wealth was a regular source of income that prevented downward wealth mobility; for other families, it meant upward wealth mobility from a large cash infusion through inheritance or gifts. Those without such a network were more likely in an emergency to take hardship withdrawals from savings and retirement accounts to pay everyday expenses. When faced with a drop in income, families without a well-resourced web of wealth were less able to protect assets such as a house or car, more likely to take their children out of private schools, and more likely to take on debt. Such families had to spend more of their regular income on everyday expenditures and thus were less likely to build up as much wealth through savings or home owner-ship. Once again, access to family financial networks varied significantly based on race.

Stressful life events such as unemployment, a downturn in health status, the onset of a disability, or the loss of a spouse can dramatically diminish family wealth accumulation.[37] As our interviews made clear, most families faced negative life events like these at some point in their lives. But some faced more than others. Black families were more likely to confront a range of different negative life events, from unemployment to a health crisis.[38] To cope with the loss of income that typ-ically resulted from a negative life event, families usually drew on saved financial assets.[39] But many families were not then able to go back to building wealth or even to maintain a new, decreased level of wealth. Often, their savings were not sufficient to manage the crisis, and families became vulnera-ble to a spiral of continuously decreasing assets, especially if they had few to start with.

Debt also negatively influenced families' capacity to save, setting them on a downward path. Families we interviewed had debts of many kinds: credit card balances, payday loans, mortgages, health-care debt, student loan debt, and car loans. Critically, the cost of the debt, more than the total owed, determined whether a family was able to avoid losing wealth. Patricia Arrora's story, described in the introduction, illustrates how important debt can be to a family's wealth mobility. Recall that Arrora had built up savings through the Family Self-Sufficiency (FSS) program, enrolled in a first-time home-buyer program and bought her first home, then sold it to purchase a larger suburban home with financing. After her husband lost his job, Patricia found herself having to pay the mortgage with her income alone. As she put it, "I was still able to pay it, but it was like I wasn't having no extra money left, and that's what caused me to use credit cards." She found it increasingly difficult to make the minimum payments and could see that if she paid only the minimum amounts, it would take her twenty-seven years to pay off what she owed. Instead of continuing to build wealth, Patricia had $7,000 of high-cost debt and was at risk of defaulting on both her credit cards and her mortgage. Instead of stabilizing her family during her husband's unemployment, reliance on high-cost credit was actually making things worse. Fortunately, she was able to get a loan modification to reduce the 17 percent interest rate on her home mortgage, and she worked with a credit counselor to consolidate her credit card payments, reducing the cost of her debt and bringing more financial stability.

In a real, concrete way, national welfare policy, through the highly successful FSS program, enabled Patricia Arrora to become a home owner and jump-started her wealth generation. An underserving program with current funding reaching nowhere near the number of eligible families, FSS helps people like Patricia move to housing stability. Approximately 2 million households living in federally subsidized housing could qualify for FSS; currently the program reaches only 72,000, which is less than 4 percent capacity. For Cindy Breslin, by contrast, welfare policies did not keep pace with her family's needs, pushing them deeper into poverty. Unfortunately, Cindy's experience is far more common than Patricia's.

Our interviews coincided with a period when American welfare policy and its impact on families' fortunes transformed substantially. In August 1996, proclaiming, "We are ending welfare as we know it," President Bill Clinton signed the Personal Responsibility and Work Opportunity Reconciliation Act, historic legislation that altered six decades of social policy, ended the federal guarantee of cash assistance to the poor, and turned welfare programs over to the states through block grants. Whereas the Aid to Families with Dependent Children program had provided cash assistance for 13 million people, only 3 million received such assistance under its replacement, Temporary Assistance for Needy Families (TANF), in 2016. The 1996 law limited people to no more than five years of government benefits, while allowing states to set their own shorter limits, which many did. It also stipulated that recipients must actively search for jobs, participate in "voluntary" community service, or seek vocational training. States had great discretion in spending their block grants and responding to unemployment and work policy.

At the time of our first interviews (1998) all our families resided in California, Massachusetts, and Missouri. Not surprisingly, these (and other) states responded with a wide array of policies to the Great Recession's surging unemployment and poverty rates. TANF assistance in California reached 17 percent more people in 2014 than in 2006, whereas in Massachusetts it covered 10 percent fewer people. California and Massachusetts retained relatively moderate welfare benefits.

Missouri took a particularly hard line, shortening the maximum benefit period from five years to three and a half and requiring people to be employed or engaged in activities like taking classes or performing community service prior to becoming eligible. These criteria probably do not even save Missouri money because the administrative cost of making sure everyone is meeting them offsets any savings. Moreover, Missouri sets 4 percent of its block grant aside for "alternatives to abortion" and "marriage promotion activities"—which have nothing to do with getting people ready for work and into decent jobs.[40]

In Missouri, the changes to welfare serve as a prime example of how the safety net has been shredded. This puts more pressure on paltry, often nonexistent, emergency savings and already stressed networks to compensate for deeper poverty. Missouri's unemployment rate in December 2006 stood at 4.9 percent; in December 2014, following the recession and stalled recovery, it had climbed to 5.5 percent. With a corollary rise in the number of families and children living in poverty, one might reasonably expect an expansion of TANF to meet the greater need. Yet, although 15,000 more unemployed people became eligible for TANF, the state's TANF's roll plummeted by 31.5 percent. Put another way, the state's TANF-to-unemployment ratio was 28.9 percent at the end of 2006; after restriction of limits and constriction of eligibility, this ratio had tumbled to 18 percent by the end of 2014.

The numbers tell a story. The part of welfare reform attractive to conservatives and those concerned that social assistance fosters dependence and laziness has achieved clear victory. Cash assistance plunged from 13 million to 5 million between 1996 and 2014. Getting people ready for work and into jobs, alleviating poverty, and accomplishing those reforms more attractive to liberals have been a dismal failure.

The Supplemental Nutrition Assistance Program (SNAP), formerly known as the Food Stamp Program, is the nation's most important antihunger initiative. After unemployment insurance, SNAP is the most responsive federal program providing additional assistance during economic downturns. It also provides important nutritional support for low-wage working families, low-income seniors, and people with disabilities living on fixed incomes. In 2015, it helped more than 45 million low-income Americans afford a nutritionally adequate diet in a typical month. Close to 70 percent of SNAP participants belong to families with children. The federal government pays for all SNAP benefits and splits the cost of administering the program with the states, which operate the program.

Unlike most means-tested benefit programs, which are restricted to particular categories of low-income individuals, SNAP is broadly available to almost all households with a gross monthly income at or below 130 percent of poverty. SNAP eligibility rules and benefit levels are, for the most part, set at the federal level and uniform across the nation, though states can tailor aspects that determine eligibility, such as asset limits (e.g., the value of a household's vehicle or college savings account).[41]

Where states like Missouri have thrown people off social assistance and deepened poverty with actions that confine

TANF eligibility and benefits, the federal government's SNAP sands down the sharpest edges by reaching more families to make food more affordable. Research shows that millions more Americans are living in deep poverty—defined as family income below 50 percent of the federal poverty line—since the 1994 grand change in welfare and subsequent state restrictions.[42] As Missouri was cutting its rolls while unemployment rose, the SNAP food assistance program provided 62,000 more Missourians with food in 2014 than it did in 2006.

OUR INTERVIEWS WITH A DIVERSE SET OF FAMILIES—BLACK, white, and Hispanic; poor, middle-class, and successful— provide a dynamic portrait of economic mobility and security in modern America that aligns with the statistical findings from nationally representative data. Wealth mobility is closely connected to location of home ownership, enabling employment structures such as workplace-based benefits, and access to networks of family wealth. Debt has a severe negative impact on wealth trajectories, especially in the absence of extended family wealth or support. The African American families we interviewed experienced more relative wealth churning, both up and down, than white families. Overall, African Americans are more likely to be stuck at the bottom and to fall from the middle of the economic ladder across a generation. We talked to many low-income, struggling black families in 1998, and the huge majority of them were still struggling with poverty in 2012.

Our interviews uncovered many success stories of families that moved out of poverty, like Patricia Arrora's.

Critical institutional and policy opportunities were key to their achievements, confirming that wealth inequality is not simply a matter of individual successes and failures. We also heard many wrenching stories about aspirations thwarted, hard work unrewarded, and dreams dashed. Many families seem to get only one chance at success. Misfortune derails progress too easily because there is not sufficient wealth to cushion setbacks or smooth the way to recovery. Exposure to real stories of mobility gained and lost, recognition of how the playing field is dramatically weighted in favor of those in the upper wealth quintiles, and insight into how barriers to African American wealth building have become baked into the economy due to continuing discrimination and policies that protect existing wealth are critical to grasping that financial failure and poverty are not manifestations of individual sins.

This chapter has focused on wealth and its lack. For most American families their home is their largest reservoir of wealth and opportunity. The next chapter introduces several home owners whose stories illustrate the importance of home and community in building wealth and shaping well-being.

= 2 =

INEQUALITY AT HOME

THE AMERICAN DREAM IS ROOTED IN HOME AND COMMUNITY. For many, home symbolizes stability and physical security; for others it signifies an investment, an identity, or a crucial mark of citizenship. A community can provide friends and neighbors, safety, parks, good schools, and a sense of belonging. Whether secured through renting, owning, or the generosity of others, home and community represent the bedrock of a family's future.

Yet not every home and community offer all of these advantages, and not everyone takes the same path home. The dream of securing a foothold of one's own can play out in vastly different ways based on race and economic circumstances. In recent years, buying a home has become more difficult. In the United States the age of first-time home buyers is about thirty-three; in the 1970s new home owners were four years younger. In 2014, the share of first-time buyers fell to its lowest point in nearly three decades: one-third of all sales. Rising rents, huge student debt burdens, limited job prospects, and flat wage growth all make putting money aside for a down payment an exceedingly problematic proposition for young adults in our post-Recession, toxic inequality era.[1]

Both wealth and race matter. Nearly 70 percent of first-time buyers were white in 2015; 9 percent were black, 14 percent were Hispanic, and 7 percent were Asian; 26 percent had received a gift or loan from parents, a relative, or a friend to make the down payment. I am convinced the actual numbers are even higher. In our interviews, nearly every home owner, whether black or white, told us how important family financial help was in pulling together down payments and being able to afford homes in the desired community. In this area, family interviews uncover critical information that broader surveys miss or vastly underreport—perhaps due to the deep tradition in American culture of seeing accomplishment as earned or deserved and thus denying that help was necessary. Even so, Zillow analysts estimated that nearly a quarter of all buyers with moderate incomes in 2014 (between $32,250 and $54,500) received financial assistance from family members. Whites received family financial assistance in home purchases more than twice as often as blacks.[2]

The high cost of home ownership is just one of the many reasons underlying the stratification of secure housing in a strong community. Becoming a home owner requires a stable income and wealth, especially as the home-price-to-income ratio has widened in recent decades. In the early 1970s a typical home cost 1.7 years of median income; by the early 2010s it cost the equivalent of 2.6 years of income. It takes wealth to become a home owner, and housing wealth in turn forms the largest financial asset for the middle 60 percent of families; home equity represents two-thirds of their wealth. The adage "wealth begets wealth" is institutionally rooted in neighborhoods and housing markets for middle-class families.[3]

The resulting financial and social gains from home ownership are vastly distorted. Toxic inequality is created, magnified, and reproduced partly through the structures through which we seek homes in neighborhoods highly segregated by income, wealth, and race, which in turn confer inequitable opportunities and financial rewards. Only some neighborhoods offer access to good schools, low violent crime rates, parks and green spaces, and quality employment opportunities and services. Home equity generally rises in these communities, particularly in high-socioeconomic-status neighborhoods. In contrast, other communities have weak or failing schools and high crime rates and are physically isolated from service and employment centers. If home values rise at all in these neighborhoods, the appreciation is considerably lower. This pattern of spatial inequality is highly racialized.[4]

Disparities in neighborhood opportunity—public school quality, crime rate, home value appreciation, access to public spaces, availability of quality employment—create divergent living contexts. Families residing in high-opportunity neighborhoods benefit from heightened prospects and well-being. In contrast, families residing in low-opportunity neighborhoods with weaker schools, limited education, low-wage employment, higher crime rates, and fewer public spaces have constrained prospects and diminished well-being. The physical structure is an important component in shaping a home's value, but neighborhood characteristics are also critical. Low community wealth and weak opportunity infrastructures like schools tend to further suppress already low housing appreciation. Meanwhile, high community wealth and strong opportunities and services are more desirable and translate into higher home prices and house appreciation.[5]

Neighborhood is the pivotal context for home. A neighborhood's opportunity quality varies considerably by both its economic and racial composition and its institutions. Those who own homes in affluent communities rich with institutions and opportunities consolidate their advantages and get ahead, whereas home owners or renters in low-opportunity or unstable neighborhoods, often due to the legacies of residential segregation, are at a serious disadvantage.[6]

Toxic inequality also means that communities in decline continue to decline while communities on the rise continue to rise, creating further and starker economic and social separation. The combination of housing patterns, a shrinking property tax base, and predominantly low-income and minority residents usually means great effort and inspiration are required to turn a community's fortunes around. Poor communities get worse and worse, while rich communities get harder and harder to break into. As communities diverge and the distance between high- and low-opportunity areas widens, inequality hardens.

FAMILY STORIES PROVIDE ONE WAY TO SHED LIGHT ON THE importance and multiple meanings of home; how families plan for mobility and build wealth through their decisions about where to live; and how neighborhoods increasingly divided by wealth and race parcel out opportunities to some and challenges to others, resulting in further inequality. Consider the unusual story of Rachel and Shawn Andrews, a professional, middle-class black family with the resources to live in a secure and opportunity-rich neighborhood. Their situation illustrates a specific dilemma many black middle-class families face: move to a more prosperous but largely white community or stay in a lower-opportunity neighborhood and negotiate weak schools, high crime, and poor services while attempting to improve community life for all. The Andrewses' decision to take the latter course dramatizes the trenchant effects that neighborhood location and community wealth can have on family fortunes. Reaching for the American dream in what seems like a paradoxical manner, the Andrewses built their home, and their lives, in a devastated, largely neglected community. Their journey to a secure home in an insecure neighborhood reveals both what a truly exceptional family can accomplish and the constraints of toxic inequality.

A line from Achmat Dangor's *Kafka's Curse* reverberates in Rachel's homestead: "It struck me that our history is contained in the homes we live in, that we are shaped by the ability of these simple structures to resist being defiled."[7]

Rachel and Shawn Andrews owned a home in a poverty-ridden North St. Louis neighborhood where very few educated, professional, middle-class families raising children would consider living. Like over 95 percent of their neighbors, they were African American. Driving through their immediate neighborhood in 1998 I imagined that only a Katrina-like disaster could have left such devastation: grass covered the empty spaces where homes once stood, broken and boarded-up windows were everywhere visible, and condemned buildings were a frequent sight. Yet these sat alongside homes that had been maintained or fixed up, occupied by families who were holding on. The balance between pockmarked decay and vibrant life changed block by block. The Andrewses' street was among the better ones—only a couple of boarded-up "zombie homes" and nine vacant lots, by my count. Large, beautiful trees shaded their three-story brick home.

Rachel was single, twenty-three years old, fresh out of graduate school, and new to St. Louis when she bought the house in 1979. She did not want to be a renter. Her parents were home owners and had taught her that homes are hedges against recessions because "jobs are never promised to you."

Housing had been tough to find when she arrived in St. Louis the year before. The city was notably segregated, and she could neither build up credit nor find anyone willing to rent to her. Discouraged, Rachel went so far as to call her father to tell him she was coming home. His response: "Do not come back home, baby. We love you but do not come home. You have money . . . find a YWCA." Taking her father's advice, Rachel lived at the Y for a short while until she was able to take over the lease of a friend who was moving to California. Less than a year later, she bought the house in which she now lived.

When asked how she chose the home, Rachel replied, "I didn't choose it, it chose me." As an urban planner, she was working on a project to develop and rehabilitate 150 affordable homes. In an impoverished, largely African American neighborhood, she found a run-down, abandoned house that her firm did not want to rehab as part of the project. It was "raggedy as hell," Rachel said, "and that's what I was looking for. . . . It had to be raggedy for me to afford it." It would become the Andrewses' homestead.

Rachel paid $1,500 in cash out of her first paycheck to buy the house and could barely afford to eat for a couple of weeks. The house had belonged to the first black morticians in St. Louis, and their children had not wanted to keep it up. It had been vacant for five years, the windows and doors covered over with tin. The owners were delighted to get rid of it because they no longer wanted to pay the taxes or cut the grass. Most of the other houses on the block looked just as run-down as Rachel's, some worse.

For Rachel, $1,500 was the price of admission into a community devastated by private disinvestment, a long history of residential segregation, and bad urban policy. Only in a hollowed-out African American neighborhood full of boarded-up homes and condemned buildings in a long-neglected part of the city could one find a three-story brick home at such a bargain price. But as low as that price might seem, home ownership remained a daunting and expensive proposition for a single young black woman on her own just starting her career. To make the house livable, Rachel needed to fix the roof, windows, plumbing, and heating system. She needed to refinish floors, tear out walls and put in new ones, renovate the kitchen and bathroom, and paint. A day after the purchase was finalized, she started with a front door. "I hung the front door the next day because it didn't have one. It had been vacant for five years," she said. Rachel recounted shoring up the house's most basic systems, one by one. The amenities came later; the luxuries, much, much later.

It was hard work, but Rachel considered herself a pioneer. She put the necessary sweat equity into making her home livable and then, in her words, "moved into the dust."

During our 1998 interview, she talked about her experience as a divorcée raising a son, the money spent on his private schooling, and society's perceptions of a black family like hers. Her marriage to Shawn—the second for both of them—was relatively new, and in many ways she still thought of herself as a single mom preoccupied with the dangers of raising a teenage boy in St. Louis. When we talked in 2010, Rachel seemed more settled, thinking of herself as a wife, a mother, a professional, a home owner, and an anchor of her community. Rachel's son from her first marriage was in his early thirties and, after a stint in the military, was working and attending nursing school full-time. Rachel and Shawn's daughter, Stephanie, was attending high school.

In 2010, the Andrews family was a bright spot of success in the midst of an otherwise impoverished neighborhood. The couple earned $125,000 in a census tract where the median income, at $17,102, was well below the poverty line. Rachel valued their home at $160,000, but they were surrounded by houses with a median sales price of $11,250. "For sale" signs and foreclosure auction notices dotted their block in a neighborhood where foreclosure affected one in eight homes. Some areas near Rachel and Shawn's house were coming back up, but St. Louis had still not quite recovered from the foreclosure crisis that devastated families and communities starting in 2007.

Rachel's home was a block north of the major east-west boulevard that racially divides St. Louis to this day. To the south of that boundary are gated streets, Tudor homes, boutiques and antique shops, restaurants, a whiskey bar, and an independent bookstore. These neighborhoods are largely white. To the north of the boulevard, one sees collapsing houses, weeds popping through cracking sidewalks, and few stores or businesses. These neighborhoods are almost all black.[8]

Indeed, one might ask why the Andrews family, with a $125,000 family income and an estimated net wealth of $630,000, remained in the same neighborhood. The average real estate broker, financial advisor, or middle-class home owner would likely be shocked at the family's choice and defiance of the tried-and-true pattern of American economic mobility of moving up by moving out. Yet African Americans have not always had this option. In the past, formal segregation prevented them from following this time-honored path, and even today segregation's legacy poses challenges that whites typically do not confront. The Andrewses were clearly capable of affording a newer, bigger home in a more upscale and stable community. Yet their home was part of their identity. It represented growth and advancement dating back to Rachel's first paycheck when it was still "raggedy as hell." Against the odds, she made that house her home. Over the years employers cut jobs and downsized or moved industries away from North St. Louis. Rachel and Shawn were fortunate in that they worked in jobs not readily cut or moved, but as urban blight spread around them, the house itself remained a safe haven and a key part of who they were, just as her parents had told her it would.

The neighborhood had become part of the Andrews family's identity as well. In the 1990s, Rachel became keenly interested in starting a block improvement association. She and her group pushed to board up vacant homes, worked to keep drug dealers out, cleaned up empty lots, fought to bring back services, and sought to set up a neighborhood watch. This intensive level of engagement was necessary to make the community livable. Rachel still remained active in the block association over a decade later, though her work had expanded to involve more communities. "I'm very entrenched in what goes on in the city of St. Louis," she said proudly in 2010. Against the standard American strategy of moving up by moving out into areas with a better school system or a private school, Rachel stayed behind to build. This commitment to improving her neighborhood made her both a pioneer and pillar of her community.

In 2010, Rachel's neighborhood was changing around her, and she remained a keen observer of the transformations. When she bought her house in 1979, there were lots of vacant homes and a large senior population. The neighborhood consisted mainly of single-family homes, a few two-family homes, and some apartment buildings. These properties had been among the first that African Americans were able to buy in St. Louis, and they had been handed down through generations. Many of the families that originally came, African American families, had attended the neighborhood schools. They knew each other because they grew up together.

In 2010, the neighborhood was slowly attracting new residents. They tended to be younger, consisting of extended families with low and moderate incomes. Rachel noticed how the neighborhood was gradually changing economically and becoming more racially diverse. She noticed a few white families, a Hispanic family, a Bosnian family, firefighters, women walking with babies, men riding bikes, and people jogging—welcome signs of a stabilizing and improving neighborhood. There was no imminent danger of the kind of gentrification that displaces longtime or older residents or uproots families. Starbucks was not likely to set up shop in the near future. Home values, rents, and property taxes were not increasing so quickly as to make the neighborhood unaffordable to current denizens.

The value of the Andrewses' home had increased with all these changes, despite the mortgage crisis and high unemployment. When we talked in 2010, Rachel thought her house would sell for about $160,000. Asked whether she viewed the equity she had built up in it as a special kind of money, she termed it "liquid," considering it equity that she could use for emergencies or collateral on a loan, a safety net. Then she told a revealing story about when she first bought the house: "The day I was hanging the door this guy drove up and said, 'I will give you $16,000 if you would sell your house to me.' I looked at him and said, 'My blood is in this house, man. I just cut my finger.' He just started laughing, and he said, 'I don't have enough for your blood.' I said, 'You sure don't.'"

The family continued to get unsolicited offers from time to time. But Rachel had no interest in selling. The home was a safety net and a hedge against inflation. If she and Shawn lost their jobs, they did not have to worry. Owning the house outright, as they had for decades, they could draw unemployment to pay their bills and live in their own home indefinitely.

But for the Andrews family, pioneering in a low-opportunity neighborhood lacking support structures came with heavy, hidden costs that the majority of middle-class and professional families never have to shoulder. Foremost among these were weak, poorly funded schools. Rachel succinctly summarized decades of social science studies with a simple observation: "Our school rolls with the housing patterns."

In the city of St. Louis, housing patterns are highly segregated by race and income, the result of a history that includes a 1916 ordinance establishing "Negro blocks," covenants restricting the buying and selling of property according to race, mobs enforcing segregation in housing and businesses, blatant discrimination by real estate agents, and a series of urban redevelopment policies, public housing measures, and zoning rules that contributed to the intense racial stratification. The city is predominantly African American, with the schools even more so. A high school eight-tenths of a mile from Rachel's home is 100 percent minority, with 95 percent of students coming from low-income families and qualifying for subsidized meals. Rachel remarked that throughout St. Louis, families with greater wealth, especially those with school-age children, have tended to move out to the suburbs, leaving a city principally consisting of lower-income renters who cannot contribute to the shrinking property tax base supporting the school system.

This situation is all the more vexing because the children of the low-income families who remain in the city are precisely those most in need of attention and resources. These families experience a complicated set of social problems, including environmentally induced asthma, lead-paint health hazards, and the other illnesses and troubles that accompany them. Yet Rachel was not without hope. In her long experience in the community, she had witnessed students perform well so long as proven supports and well-resourced programs were in place both at home and at school to help them. In 2007 Rachel developed a tutoring program for students that were failing in schools and watched as math and language scores improved dramatically. "The resources and money isn't there for lower-income students," but they succeeded on Missouri statewide performance assessment tests "because an additional resource is in place to give them what they need." She also pointed to "lighthouses" within the system, schools like the magnet school for bright, high-performing students that her daughter Stephanie attended, where "there's little rays of hope." Rachel proudly reported, "It's the number one school in the state of Missouri and it's maybe the number fourteen school out of the top one hundred in the nation." Performance assessment tests indicate that just 15.5 percent of St. Louis high schoolers are college ready, while 78 percent are college ready at Stephanie's school; 29 percent of students district-wide are proficient in English, compared to 91 percent at Stephanie's high school.[9] Stephanie's school has less than half the students of many of the other St. Louis high schools; 58 percent are students of color, and 40 percent come from low-income families, both considerably lower figures than for other St. Louis schools. The day before Rachel and I talked in 2010, the school superintendent had announced that there would be no further teacher and school personnel layoffs that year. But three years later, facing yet another periodic budget squeeze, several more city schools were closed down, teachers let go, and class sizes increased.[10]

Rachel Andrews is a jewel any community would be proud to claim in its crown of assets. Her vision, since first hanging her front door in 1979, has rested on the increased prosperity of the neighborhood, allowing the Andrewses to stay in place. Instead of moving to a bigger house in a safer community with a richer educational environment and treating their home only as a financial investment, they stayed put, pioneered change, and navigated weak infrastructures of opportunity so that they and their children would not have to take on all the disadvantages of their community. Perhaps because of her St. Louis experiences, talents, and character, Rachel Andrews counts her blessings and wants to take her community-building talents and wisdom global, to something like the Peace Corps, when she retires. "God blessed me with tools and talents. . . . I've always felt that I should share what I have. I've never been without. . . . I can only imagine." Because she has witnessed "being without" in the lives of others, she says, "If there's something that I can give and I can be of service, I am."

IT IS NO GRAND REVELATION THAT SOME NEIGHBORHOODS offer resources that make them more desirable than others. Most families would prefer to live in neighborhoods with good schools, low crime rates, stable or rising home values, nearby employment opportunities, trees, parks and recreation, accessible transportation, and reliable services such as police, fire, and garbage collection. Such high-opportunity neighborhoods have obvious advantages over those with failing schools, high crime rates, declining or unstable home values, poor services, and few employment prospects.

Families living in high-opportunity neighborhoods see real gains in financial, social, and physical well-being. Children who attend high-quality public schools receive more resources, support, opportunities, and encouragement; they also have higher peer expectations of graduating high school and attending college. Neighborhoods with low violent and property crime rates reduce the risks of physical and mental harm. Neighborhoods with stable or rising property prices increase the likelihood of household wealth growing through home equity. Neighborhoods with nearby employment mean less time spent commuting and increased opportunities for work. Transportation, whether public or private, ensures that families have easy access to employment and other amenities.

In contrast, those living in low-opportunity neighborhoods with poor-quality schools and high crime rates face challenge after challenge—less home-value appreciation, fewer physical and mental health services, lower educational outcomes— inhibiting their capacity to live well and move ahead. Students attending schools with high concentrations of poverty have worse educational outcomes.[11] Residents of low-opportunity neighborhoods are likely to pay more for groceries and services, as well as higher auto insurance premiums and mortgage rates. Such neighborhoods generally provide fewer local job prospects, and many have poor transit connections to growing job centers. Finding better employment is also harder because neighbors all tend to work the same kind of jobs offering neither secure employment nor opportunities to move up the ladder.

Communities with low or weak opportunities are often vulnerable in ways we do not think about, especially if they are communities of color. Legal judgments stemming from debt-collection lawsuits (usually small consumer debts) are clustered in black neighborhoods.[12] An exhaustive study of such settlements in three cities over five years of court actions found that judgments were twice as high in black neighborhoods, even after controlling for neighborhood income. The study concluded that generations of racial discrimination, along with fewer resources to navigate personal, health, or family crises, contributed to black families' heightened financial vulnerability. Such stumbling blocks blight the lived experiences and budgets of families of color; yet they are invisible to those who live in white neighborhoods.

Parents universally express a strong desire to move into safe areas with good schools, realizing that neighborhood and peers can impact their own and their children's life trajectories.[13] While these outcomes are compelling, perceptions of quality and opportunity play an important role in residential choice. Although families are drawn to and choose neighborhoods within their budgets for many different reasons, most would indisputably prefer to live in an attractive, high-opportunity neighborhood where they can grow and thrive. To a large extent families know what they are talking about, and, indeed, they vote with moving vans. As families move, they help to both construct and reinforce these very patterns of neighborhood opportunity.

In short, neighborhoods in the United States are not created equal. As in St. Louis, although perhaps not always in as stark a fashion, dividing lines of color and wealth across the country are the living legacies of segregation, redlining, discriminatory local ordinances, steering by realtors, private disinvestment, and public policy choices. Adding to residential segregation, neighborhoods are becoming increasingly segregated by the quality of the resources and opportunities they offer. At the same time that income and wealth inequality has reached historic levels, the chasm between high- and low-opportunity neighborhoods has widened. Instant communication and social media connections cannot span our growing physical, social, and opportunity divides.

As the high- and low-opportunity divide sharpens, and as low-opportunity areas become more numerous, more families are living in concentrated poverty. The interview team witnessed this growing trend among the families in Boston, Los Angeles, and St. Louis. Since 1970, the number of high-poverty neighborhoods in the United States has tripled, and the number of poor people living in them has doubled. Due partly to the Great Recession, 5 million more Americans lived in highly distressed neighborhoods in 2012 than did so before 2006.[14] One report looking at neighborhood inequality examined urban areas from 1970 to 2010 and found that census tracts populated by about 4 million people in total slumped from below the poverty line to high poverty (30 percent or more below the poverty line) during these decades.[15] While living in poverty is difficult and challenging anywhere, it is made worse when a large fraction of one's neighbors are also poor.

Fewer than one in ten high-poverty neighborhoods in 1970 cut their poverty rates by more than half by 2010.[16] Three times as many communities are joining the ranks of high-poverty neighborhoods as are escaping this sort of distress, indicating that we are headed in the wrong direction. Economically segregated neighborhoods inhibit family economic mobility more than inequality, per se.[17] The double whammy here is that individual and location-based inequality are integrally connected, and both are increasing. Understanding neighborhood inequality is critical to deepen our understanding of wealth, poverty, and chances for mobility not because neighborhoods group families economically but because opportunities, networks, and services pass advantage and challenges along. Despite beacons of success like the Andrews family, the clear trend is toward neighborhood economic decline and segregation.

Many families cannot realize the dream of living in a high-opportunity neighborhood. A family's wealth determines the choices available in maximizing neighborhood quality. While some families can draw on a rich set of resources to gain access to high-opportunity neighborhoods, parents with few resources are more often stuck in low-opportunity neighborhoods and cannot afford to pay privately for services like schooling or safety. These disparities in resources, which vary heavily depending on race and class, mean that race and class sort families into starkly different neighborhoods. The story of Freda Harmon offers a glimpse of what it is like to be trapped in a low-opportunity neighborhood without the benefit of the middle-class resources the Andrews family enjoyed. In Freda's experience, we find challenges and choices most middle-class families would hardly recognize.

FREDA HARMON, A SINGLE MOTHER, HAD LIVED IN LOW-opportunity Boston neighborhoods all her life. Since we first spoke in 1998 she had moved six times, trying to find a safer neighborhood for herself and her three children. By 2010, because she could not afford to live anywhere else, she was renting in a neighborhood with regular gang presence, shootings, and robberies. "A lot of murders around the corner. I can be in my house [and] I hear gunshots at 2:00 in the afternoon," Freda vividly recalled. In neighborhoods like hers, violence and fear are not confined to the streets. Freda remarked that "parks are supposed to be for kids to play, but if you don't have the police patrolling these areas to make sure this is happening, anything can happen." She remembered a little girl who was murdered. "It's supposed to be a park where kids can play," she lamented.

Fearing for the safety of her three children, two years earlier Freda had left her full-time job as a medical assistant in a suburban doctor's office for more flexible hours working in customer service at a grocery store. The new job allowed her to be closer to home and to her children's schools, enabling her to better protect her family, but it also paid $8 per hour less. Freda told her children not to play outside and took other precautions out of fear that a stray bullet might strike one of them. In an effort to navigate the poorly resourced local schools, she had put her seven-year-old in therapy to address poor academic performance, attempted to place her twelve-year-old in a program that might produce a scholarship to a private school, and moved her eldest son into an alternative charter school.

Some might ask why Freda didn't move her family to safety and a strong community. If it were simply a matter of choice, she might have done so already. But she could not afford the rent anywhere else. The affordability constraint aside, moving would also take a kind of emotional toll, undermining her pride in the place she had made home. Freda said, "Every time I want a new, big kitchen, curtains. Some apartments don't have curtains. The bathroom . . . I usually do it over. It cost money to move. So I'm like damn, I guess I can't move again. I try to stay here. I've been here two years. So I'm tired of moving." Place is neither fate nor legacy, but Freda knew its power firsthand. "Sometimes you can just be at the wrong place at the wrong time," she said. "But this is not the wrong place 'cause we live here."

The average income of families living in a neighborhood is a close indicator of its quality and opportunity. In 2010, nearly half of white families in America lived in high-opportunity neighborhoods, as compared to about one-fifth of African American families.[18] These locational patterns are not simply a consequence of family income differences, however.[19] Middle-income African American families with children live in very different neighborhoods than their white counterparts. In 2000, compared to African American families with similar incomes, white families lived in neighborhoods with much higher home ownership rates (74 versus 57 percent) and higher median home values ($150,726 versus $129,170), as well as more college-educated families (24 percent with a bachelor's degree or higher versus 17 percent) and higher median incomes of neighbors ($67,672 versus $51,565). By 2010, the distance in median home values in the neighborhoods of middle-income African American and white families had increased by $18,811; the breach in college-educated families increased by 22 percent; the gap among neighbors' median incomes also ticked up. Only the gap in home ownership rates closed, largely because of an increase in black home ownership.[20] It is difficult for low-income families like the Harmons to succeed in the neighborhood where they reside; yet even middle-income African Americans continue to live disproportionately in low-opportunity neighborhoods.

Persons of color bear the burden of concentrated poverty unevenly. In 2010, African American and Latino families accounted for three-fourths of poor families living in urban neighborhoods with concentrated poverty. In that year, African Americans were eight times more likely than white residents to live in high-poverty neighborhoods, and Latinos were five times more likely.[21] These high-poverty concentrations create low-opportunity neighborhoods with severely diminished prospects.

Freda Harmon's family was poor, with little choice but to live in a low-opportunity neighborhood. The larger picture shows that regardless of income, black families are more likely to live in such neighborhoods or in bordering communities that often share schools and public services. A third family's story suggests another reason why that is true: because extending a long historical pattern, these neighborhoods become weaker and more poorly resourced. The story of these places is deeply rooted in past and present policy. To

show how seemingly abstract explanations like residential racial dynamics, active real estate churning, and tipping points
can affect a family's arc and contribute to toxic inequality
and the racial wealth gap, we turn to the Medinas.

THE MIDDLE-CLASS MEDINA FAMILY MOVED TO THE DIVERSI-
fying municipality of Spanish Lake in northeastern St. Louis
County in 1998. Spanish Lake was long ago an embarkation
spot for the Lewis and Clark expedition. Bounded by the
Mississippi River to the east, the Missouri River to the north,
and highways to the west and south, the 7.5-square-mile
Spanish Lake was once a model 1950s white working-class
community. Over the years, however, its fortunes have fallen.
Spanish Lake now represents a classic case of residential segregation, poor federal housing policy, and white flight.

In 1998, India Medina described what drew her to the
house she liked in Spanish Lake: it was spacious, with a wide-
open kitchen, and in the family's price range. The neighborhood was really good, with a professor and his kids living next
door. India emphasized how "everybody kind of was owning
and stuff." Yet over the ensuing decade, real estate brokers,
speculators, and predatory lenders seized upon a vulnerable
moment and transformed the community for the worse.

Spanish Lake may have fit the Medina family's budget in
1998, but by 2010 it didn't suit their needs or aspirations.
They were not happy with the schools, but finding a community with quality schools, given their moderate resources,
had proven difficult. Such a move, India said, "requires that
we spend more money [on a home]. The correlation is, the

more money you have, the better school district you're going to be in."

The neighborhood changed quickly after the Medinas moved in. Once anchored by a diverse set of home owners, by 2010 it consisted mostly of renters. As India explained it, "They've Sectioned Eight a lot of these houses [provided rent subsidies for low-income families]. . . . [T]he brokers have bought them up when the people moved out." India witnessed firsthand the white flight as the neighborhood tipped from owners to subsidized renters, from white to black. "Black people start moving in, white people start moving out, and then the neighborhood kind of was crashing down," India said. There is hardly any diversity left, and now most of the community's residents, like the Medinas, are black.

Alongside this demographic transformation, the Medina family's home value sank quickly from $100,000 to $70,000. When we spoke to her in 2010, India believed it was undervalued and hoped that it would come back up. But hope was in short supply, and she seriously doubted the house's value would rise. This had ominous financial implications. When we asked about the money the family had put into the house, India said, "Oh, yeah. Yeah, we can't get our money out of this house now." The Medinas contemplated following the white flighters who had departed before them. "We'll probably be forced to do the same thing everybody else does, it's rent it out," India said. "Sell it out to a broker and let them rent it out, or rent it out ourselves."

India was clear about who she blamed for transforming and destroying her neighborhood: real estate speculators and absentee owners. "They're renting out houses," she said.

"You're kind of destroying the whole structure of things, and I just don't think you can bring the neighborhood back with people moving in and out, in and out." Indeed, America's number one home owner today is not an owner-occupant but one of the world's largest and most successful private equity companies: Blackstone Group. With almost 50,000 single-family homes acquired since the housing crisis, it is fair to say that no single entity in history has placed a bigger bet on the US housing market. Financial speculators like Blackstone buy homes at depressed, often foreclosure, prices, perhaps spruce them up, and then rent them out, offering a rent-to-own scheme. Some utilize federal rental subsidies,[22] the kind India referred to as Section Eight, and rent to low-income families. In Spanish Lake the landlords tended to be smaller hedge fund investment firms.[23] Private equity firms, hedge funds, real estate investment trusts, and other institutional investors spent more than $20 billion to buy as many as 200,000 rental homes in the United States between 2012 and 2014. They snapped up properties as housing prices fell as much as 35 percent from the 2006 peak and rental demand rose as a result of the almost 5 million owners who had gone through foreclosure since 2008.[24] Blackstone and others transform hamlets like Spanish Lake from communities of owner-occupied homes into blocks of renters and absentee landlords.

Rapid neighborhood transition like that which occurred in Spanish Lake causes devastating upheavals in families and communities. Speculators, real estate brokers, and financial investment firms purchase homes at bargain prices and profit at the expense of community stability as home owners are forced out, in many cases their life savings wiped out. Absentee landlords hold on to the properties, hoping they will increase in value as times get better, while benefiting from federal rent subsidies. And communities where the Medinas and families like them had hoped to lay the foundation for getting ahead have instead become low-opportunity areas. Before its rapid transition, India said in 2010, Spanish Lake had been a place where people stayed for a long time and someone like her could develop sustainable relationships and networks. But now, she did not see the neighborhood coming back; instead she saw it getting worse. "We aren't staying."

As neighborhood opportunity segregation widens and hardens, the rewards or disadvantages of community location become more visible. Families we spoke to like the Medinas seemed to understand this dynamic implicitly, and if they had the financial resources, most intentionally sought better-resourced and higher-opportunity locations. But most families who want to move to these neighborhoods find the costs prohibitive as access typically requires home ownership. Some who cannot afford the high real estate prices and property taxes common in these communities seek other ways of securing their unique benefits. They need to navigate schools and services, bearing the often hidden costs of seeking better opportunities.

RESEARCH SUGGESTS THAT ECONOMICALLY SEGREGATED neighborhoods harden advantage and disadvantage by making economic mobility more difficult.[25] The families we interviewed were enmeshed in the central dynamic that high

geographic inequality is an additional mechanism by which
parents transmit economic advantage and disadvantage to
children, leading to lower overall levels of economic mobility. For example, the Los Angeles metro area has high
economic segregation and lower mobility. Boston has lower
economic segregation relative to many other metro areas
and slightly higher economic mobility. These findings suggest that it is harder to climb up the economic ladder in
areas that are more highly stratified economically, like Los
Angeles, where wealthy parents are more able to pass along
advantages to their children, than in more economically integrated areas like Boston.[26] While this finding is cold com-
fort for working Bostonians, especially for families of color
in a city with high levels of residential segregation, it bol-
sters the notion that greater equity improves prospects for
well-being and economic mobility. Greater inequity among
neighborhoods solidifies toxic inequality because it decreases opportunities and chances for enhanced economic
mobility for families.

Understanding their resource-laden opportunities, some
high-opportunity communities are seeking to protect their
competitive advantages—perhaps none more notoriously
than Orinda, California, in 2014.[27] Located just east of Berkeley, Orinda is home to many affluent suburban professionals
who commute to downtown Oakland, San Francisco, and
Walnut Creek. *Forbes* named it the second-friendliest town
in America in 2012, based on its 90 percent home ownership
rate, low crime, and highly educated citizens—the picture of
a high-opportunity neighborhood. Orinda's public schools
are known for their academic excellence, and their perfor-

mance scores are near the top. Striving parents, however, cannot simply enroll their children in Orinda's public school system. Home ownership is the price of admission. In early 2015, the median Orinda home price was $1.25 million, or one could rent for $4,250 a month.[28] With a median income of $164,000, Orinda is 82 percent white, compared to 57 percent of California as a whole.

In 2014, Vivian, a seven-year-old Latina, was thrown out of Orinda's public schools because a private detective hired by the school system determined that her family did not officially reside there. Vivian stayed with her mother, a live-in nanny for an Orinda family. Her case highlighted school officials' limited sense of the "public" they served—although she stayed with her mother in the community where her mother lived and worked, because Vivian and her mother could never live in Orinda on their own, Vivian was seen as a trespasser, poaching a community resource to which she was not entitled. Vivian had crossed an invisible border, gaining richer educational resources without proper documentation. Her citizenship was not questioned; her address was. After a flurry of negative news reports, Orinda relented, and Vivian is back with her schoolmates.

Orinda's methods may be exceptional—pursuit of a nanny by a private detective—but resource hoarding of this sort is becoming a standard practice in many communities. In 2011, for instance, Kelley Williams-Bolar, an African American single mother, was arrested, charged with felony larceny, and sent to jail for stealing resources from Copley Township school district in Ohio, all because she sent her two daughters to the predominantly white suburban public school without meeting the township's residency requirements.[29] The Williams-Bolar family lived in an Akron, Ohio, housing project, where the dearth of good schooling options spurred Kelley to ask her father to use his address to enroll her children in his local school instead. Her children attended the school for two years until the school district filed criminal charges against her. As in Orinda, the school district spent thousands of dollars to hire a private detective to stop her from "stealing an education." Due to public outcry, Kelley was ultimately released from jail, but the conviction stood and, as the judge harshly reprimanded, disqualified her from ever fulfilling her dream of becoming a teacher.

Stories like Kelley's reflect parents' high aspirations for their children and the lengths they will go to in an attempt to secure access to neighborhoods and schools that poise their children for a brighter future. We interviewed several families who used another family member's home address or lied about where they lived to gain access to better schools. None faced criminal charges, although one student was removed from a school system because the child's parents falsified an address. As the growing cleavages between high- and low-opportunity neighborhoods become demonstrably clear, and as the latter grow in number, moving from the latter to the former is growing ever harder. The Orinda and Copley Township resource hoarding reinforces the importance of place and wealth to opportunity. As toxic inequality rises, we will see more and more such conflicts, with all of their fraught racial politics. The California and Ohio cases serve as cautionary tales that inequality has become so toxic that crossing lines between poor and rich, between high- and low-opportunity neighborhoods, especially when it involves families of color, is potentially criminalized as a way to protect privilege.

RESIDENTS' CONCERNS AND OFFICIALS' RESOURCE HOARDING in high-opportunity communities contrast sharply with public policies in places like Ferguson, Missouri. In 1998 we talked to Linda Diamond. Then living in the heart of urban St. Louis, Linda was working hard, raising three children, and striving to move forward. Like other parents with young children, she aspired to a better life for her family and was willing to sacrifice so her children might advance. We asked where she would go if she could move anywhere. Linda hesitated. "I really haven't given a thought to it." But she quickly warmed to the idea. "I guess I'd like somewhere in the county most likely," she said. "Like Ferguson." When I asked what she liked about Ferguson, she said, "It's like, they have good schools out there." Anything else? "Just the area. It's convenient; it's like, shopping malls, stores."

Later in our conversation, again pinpointing Ferguson as her dream destination, Linda drew a connection between good schools and diversity. Linda thought that mixing with more children of different ethnic groups would be important to her children's future, because it "teaches them to get along with other people, even though their skin color is different." Like Linda, whites and African Americans alike want their children to experience diversity in schools, although the threshold for what constitutes racial integration differs dramatically by ethnic group. Diversity as defined by whites, as opposed to members of other racial or ethnic groups, involves a much lower percentage of minority group members living in their neighborhoods and attending their schools. The number of black residents at which African Americans consider a neighborhood diverse far exceeds the threshold at which most whites consider the proportion out of balance and decide to exit.[30]

This is precisely what happened in Ferguson, Missouri, Linda Diamond's dream destination in 1998. Ferguson acquired a much more tragic reputation in 2014, when a white policeman shot and killed an unarmed black teenager, Michael Brown, there. The following weeks witnessed increasing tension, demonstrations, arrests, and hostility that turned violent at times. After a grand jury refused to indict the police officer, the Black Lives Matter national movement coalesced with Ferguson as a symbol of the criminal justice system's mistreatment of African Americans. Demonstrations, lawsuits, Department of Justice investigations, and local commissions ensued. All helped to reveal how the roots of the fatal encounter between Michael Brown and the officer reached deep into the interaction between public policy, race, and a rapidly transitioning community.[31]

Ferguson, like many similar towns, including Spanish Lake, looks very different today than it did ten or twenty years ago, certainly different than the ideal Linda Diamond had in mind in 1998. In 1990, whites constituted 74 percent of the population, but that figure had plummeted to 29 percent by 2010. Blacks grew from 29 to 67 percent of the population over the same period. Many black families that moved to

Ferguson were just achieving middle-class status by virtue of their income, occupation, home ownership, and education. Many were fleeing hollowed-out sections of urban St. Louis and North St. Louis, looking for suburban safety, good homes, better schools, shops, and opportunities. In 2011, 60 percent of Ferguson residents were home owners.

Home values in Ferguson plunged in the wake of the Great Recession and the massive outbreak of foreclosures that followed, and the city's many first-time home buyers suffered. In late 2014, home values were still 40 percent below 2006 levels. In early 2015, close to three hundred homes in Ferguson were on the market; alarmingly, 70 percent were in foreclosure proceedings or had been foreclosed. Today, banks are foreclosing on Ferguson homes at four and a half times the national rate, whereas many communities experiencing similar drastic declines in home values are well along the road to recovery. Just a few miles from Ferguson, across Highway I-70, home values in many communities are at or near pre-2006 prices. These communities tend to be largely white and middle-class or wealthier.

Ferguson's 2015 median family income was $37,000, above the official poverty line but just below the level defined as middle income. Ferguson's median income was more than twice that of the inner-city St. Louis neighborhood where the Andrews family lives. Yet even high-income African American and Hispanic/Latino borrowers were more likely than similarly situated white borrowers to go into foreclosure in the wake of the recession, controlling for key financial variables. Studies examining communities like Prince

George's County, Maryland, show that the foreclosure crisis devastated many previously upwardly mobile African American and Hispanic/Latino families and, as a consequence, distressed many communities of color.[32] Borrowers of color disproportionately received mortgages on predatory terms that studies have shown made foreclosures more likely.[33]

As white flight rapidly transformed Ferguson from majority white to majority black, the municipality also began to rely more and more on fees from traffic and moving violations, as well as court fees, to finance local government. In 1980, Missouri passed the Hancock Amendment, which restructured how municipalities could raise revenues by putting severe limits on state and local property taxes. Intended or not, this measure radically changed the way cities and municipalities raised revenues, shifting from taxes levied on property owners to user and service fees, which remained unaffected by the amendment. By 2014, revenues resulting from traffic and moving violations accounted for almost a quarter of Ferguson's revenue. Fifty-five patrolmen wrote more than 14,000 traffic violations in 2013. In some real ways, police became tax collectors, trolling for and extracting municipal fines, raising revenues for the city by routinely stopping cars and issuing tickets. The tax burden fell increasingly on working-class citizens utilizing public infrastructures like streets and essential city services, shifting away from home owners, businesses, and the Fortune 500 corporation Emerson Electric, which is headquartered there.[34] As Ferguson became blacker and poorer and opportunities for its residents diminished, the old-guard city leaders increasingly raised revenue from those who could least afford to contribute.

We spoke to Linda Diamond again in early 2011. Her oldest son was working on his general equivalency diploma, her middle son was attending a local community college, and her sixteen-year-old daughter, Abby, was a high school junior planning for college. Linda's family fortunes, like those of so many others, had been a roller coaster. Her income, at poverty levels in 1998, skyrocketed all the way to her $150,000 salary as an executive chef in 2008. Her success came to an end, however, when her younger son, afflicted with sickle-cell anemia, had a stroke, and she needed to leave her high-paying job to care for him until he started doing better. Working two jobs in 2011, she brought in less than half of her 2008 income. As fortune would have it, she had never ended up moving to Ferguson. For a short time, Linda and her family moved into a rental house less than two miles from that city, but juggling several jobs and tending to a child with acute and chronic medical needs, she found keeping up a house too burdensome. Linda moved back to urban St. Louis, not far from where we first met in 1998, hoping to save money to start a business.

Then tragedy struck. In late 2011, just before Thanksgiving, a stray bullet hit Abby Diamond. A shot from a vacant lot across the street tore through windows and walls, piercing the teen's back. She died in her own home in her aunt's arms.

As if grieving was not already hard enough, the family was stuck living in the apartment, where evidence of that horrible day remained indelible on the floor. To no avail, Abby's mother and aunt tried several home remedies—bleach, milk, hydrogen peroxide, and water—to erase the bloody stain that served as a constant reminder of the girl's death. The

Diamonds planned to move as soon as they could. Just as the dream of Ferguson had turned into a nightmare for many who had moved to that community, the move back to St. Louis led to tragedy for Linda Diamond and her family.

Success and tragedy, optimism and desperation, are bound together in the stories of home that the Andrews, Harmon, Medina, and Diamond families shared with us. Some started in poverty; some were middle-class; all were African American. Some had moved many times in the period between our two interviews; some had not. No matter their specific choices, all faced greater hurdles in neighborhood opportunities, mobility, and well-being than they would have had they been white or wealthier. All of them faced advantage and disadvantage, opportunity and challenge, that hinged on their neighborhood location and community assets. In particular, opportunities allocated through neighborhoods are becoming increasingly disparate and crucial to success. Economics and race generate increasing separation between neighborhoods, with race conferring additional disadvantages even for families of color with comparable economic status.

Yet home is not the only source of opportunity, and community is not the only platform for, or stumbling block to, advancement. The next chapter moves from city streets and suburban lawns to the workplace, revealing how toxic inequality develops on the job.

=3=

INEQUALITY AT WORK

A GOOD JOB CAN PROVIDE AN AMPLE PAYCHECK, BUT THE best jobs offer much more. By affording a way to build wealth and economic security, a quality job allows the holder to optimize her family's health and welfare, to purchase and maintain a home or secure stable rental housing, and to save for a comfortable and dignified retirement. Along the way, working fosters a sense of self-worth and contributes to the health of a community. Yet, just as work propels well-being for some, it also drives inequality. The rising earnings of a relative few are one major source of the highest levels of economic inequality since the 1930s. Just as important, however, are the potential wealth gains associated with work. As crucial as work is, our contemporary employment landscape has accelerated toxic inequality.

Today, the quality of work and the benefit structures and wealth-building pathways that jobs provide diverge sharply along lines of occupation and employment sector. Increasingly, there are two classes of jobs—those that build and preserve wealth and those that keep working families stuck in place. Jobs in the first category usually provide higher incomes and regular employment, but they also offer benefits such as paid sick leave, dependent care, health care, and structured savings or retirement plans, all of which have become keys to family prosperity. Jobs on the other end of the spectrum don't just provide lower wages and less regular work; they also offer none of those keys. For example, about two of every five workers (39 percent), when sick, must either go to work regardless or stay home without pay and risk losing their jobs; 87 percent of high-wage workers have paid sick days, but only one in five low-wage workers does. Consistent work, job flexibility, and work-based resources and benefits enable families to build and protect wealth—but only some jobs provide what can be called "employment capital."[1]

Employment also widens the racial wealth gap. The pathways to well-being and wealth that jobs offer diverge along racial lines, and access to employment capital differs depending on race. Black families are more vulnerable than white families to disruptions in employment and continue to be concentrated in jobs that pay less and offer fewer wealth-building opportunities. This, in turn, undermines their prospects for building wealth over the life course. The stories of the Ackermans and the Medinas reveal the power of work in shaping families' futures.

ALLISON AND DAVID ACKERMAN WERE BOTH THIRTY-THREE years old when we spoke to them in 1998. Married for ten years, they were raising three youngsters, ages six, three, and two. They had lived in St. Louis's South County their entire lives. Jobs in human resources and public safety at large universities provided a 1998 family income of $83,000, placing them solidly in the middle class. Taking equity from their first fixer-upper home and adding some parental financial assistance, they had bought a modest three-bedroom brick house in a new development in 1990. They held a few stocks and mutual funds, had a savings account, owned a boat, and were vested in workplace pension plans, all of which brought their financial assets to about $90,000, not including their home equity.

Twelve years later, Allison and David had experienced setbacks, but their financial footing nevertheless remained firm, and their children were thriving. Their oldest son, Peter, was a sophomore in college; their daughters, Emily and Kate, were in high school and planning to follow their older brother to college. Their $125,000 combined family income had more than kept pace with inflation—rare among American families—and the Ackermans enjoyed $10,000 more in purchasing power in 2010 than they did in 1998. They still lived in the same house, and the family's financial wealth had risen to $368,000, excluding home equity. Their work-based retirement plans provided their largest wealth reserve by far. Other financial assets included modest savings accounts, their children's college accounts, and a vacation home in the Ozarks. All in all, life had been good to the Ackerman family.

Allison still worked at the same university, now as an accounting manager. Her employer provided a robust benefit package, including pension and health-care plans. Allison's employment capital enabled her children to get ahead in life. Her employee benefits provided financial assistance for them to attend any school they chose, paying up to half the cost of tuition at her private university, which fully covered Peter's tuition at the University of Missouri. "We have been extremely lucky," the couple acknowledged.

David's career took a different path. Over time, he steadily assumed greater and greater responsibilities for four different employers. Starting as a public safety dispatcher, he rose to manage an emergency joint dispatch center for safety communications for the county. Yet David's steady twenty-four-year ascent collapsed in 2010. Two weeks before we spoke to him, he had lost his job of seven years. David blamed "politics"—a newly elected mayor in one of the municipalities wanted someone else in his position. David was still digesting the job loss and figuring out his next steps, but he was not worried. As he was collecting unemployment insurance, with another family member working full-time at good wages and with assets that provided an ample protective cushion, two weeks without a paycheck was not stressing the family.

With the economy downsizing on the heels of the Great Recession and an uneven job recovery heavily tilted toward low-wage jobs, David Ackerman joined millions of other Americans in confronting the challenge of finding new work and replacing lost income. David ended up spending half a year unemployed—much longer than he anticipated. His new job, supervising communications and records at the safety department of a public institution, offered less responsibility and paid considerably less. In the decade since 2006, one-third of all households experienced unemployment, and, like David, most people who lost their jobs returned to work at lower wages. Situations like David's are increasingly common, and David's unemployment was painful for him and challenging for his family. Yet Allison's employment capital and the assets the Ackermans had built over their careers prevented it from becoming a disaster. Many other families aren't so lucky.

Through David's experience the Ackermans witnessed how work is becoming less stable and more contingent for many Americans. They also noticed their community changing. When they bought their home in 1990, their South County subdivision was new, and the community was solidly middle-class by any measure of income and occupation. But a changing economy and stalled living standards on a national level reverberated locally. Appraising his neighborhood in 2010, David said, "You know, I don't know that I know the definition of middle class anymore, but I would think it's probably . . . middle working class."

Statistically, the Ackermans remained members of the middle class, but once David took his new, lower-paying job, the family's income purchased less than it did when we first talked to them in 1998. Allison and David felt this squeeze acutely. David, like 85 percent of middle-class Americans polled in a 2012 survey, said it was more difficult to maintain living standards than it had been ten years earlier.[2] A little more than six in ten middle-class families reported having had to cut back household spending. Today, it is both harder to get into the middle class and harder to stay there than at any time since World War II. One recent study found that the middle class—defined as the share of families earning between two-thirds of and twice the national median income, or between $42,000 and $126,000 in 2014 dollars—had shrunk from 61 to 49 percent of the population since the 1970s.[3] Middle-class economic insecurity increased by 42 percent from 2004 to 2010, as measured by family assets.[4] The Great Recession accelerated a major shift toward middle-class insecurity, one that the Ackermans experienced personally.

Nevertheless, when it came to building wealth, the Ackermans were a success story. They were among the ninety-seven families we talked to whose wealth increased between 1998 and 2012, and their jobs were crucial to their gains. Perhaps most important, Allison's employer took a mandatory 5 percent pretax contribution from her salary and invested it in a defined contribution retirement account. For every dollar Allison contributed, her employer added $1.70 more. In David's work career, a couple of his employers also offered similar retirement accounts. As a result, over twenty years of working, the Ackermans had accumulated more than $350,000 in workplace-based retirement assets. This kind of automatic, matched savings mechanism is central to how American families "save" money and generate wealth. Over half of the wealth builders we talked to had access to some sort of employer-matched savings scheme, a centerpiece of the employment capital provided by the best jobs.

For all the difficulties they faced in the wake of the Great Recession—temporary job loss, lowered wages, and a slumping neighborhood—in real ways the Ackermans represent a model of family well-being and success in passing opportunities and social status along to their children. Quality jobs that provided access to employment capital were crucial. Such jobs, however, have become more the exception than the rule among American workers.

The crucial role of employment capital becomes clear when we compare the Ackermans' experience with that of India and Elijah Medina, the middle-class Spanish Lake family introduced in the previous chapter. In contrast to the Ackermans, the Medinas had weak employment capital. Although India and Elijah had skill sets similar to Allison and David, they worked for a series of small organizations and firms at lower-paying jobs that did not provide the same sort of ample health insurance, structured and matched retirement plans, and financial support for children's postsecondary education. India was a bookkeeper, and Elijah worked at two service jobs, one with a national restaurant chain. Elijah also collected, refurbished, and sold boats as a side business. Between 1998 and 2010, their actual family income increased from $50,000 to $62,000, also placing them in the middle class. These income gains came through great effort: the hard work needed to earn regular raises and promotions, Elijah's decision to take on a second job, and added income earned through self-employment. Nevertheless, the Medinas' 2010 paychecks really represented a decline in living standards because their earnings had not kept pace with inflation.

Moreover, the Medinas had built up far fewer assets than the Ackermans. Their routine expenses were higher, in no small part because India's employer's contribution toward the cost of family health insurance coverage was considerably less than that of the Ackermans' employers. The Medinas had tried to save by setting money aside, but their retirement accounts were neither mandatory nor matched by their employer. Like many other American families encountering tough times without the benefits of substantial employment capital, they tapped these small nest egg accounts to weather several family crises. As a result, in 2010 the Medinas had about $12,000 in retirement accounts, mostly in one India started a few years earlier; she wished she had started it even sooner. None of the Medinas' employers offered college savings plans or other assistance for children's education. When we talked in 1998, India and Elijah's youngest daughter, Tina, had college aspirations, but the couple's employers did not provide the support that might allow the family to realize that dream. (Research has shown that children whose families have even small amounts of dedicated college savings are three times more likely to attend college.[5]) In 2010, Tina was not college bound; she worked as a receptionist at a local hotel. When we asked about Tina's plans for college, India was not optimistic: "[Tina] says she plans to go back to school, but we'll see."

When we spoke to them in 2010, the Ackermans expressed great confidence in the future, with $350,000 in their retirement accounts and the means to put their children through college. The Medinas were anxious, especially about what getting older would mean for them. Peter Ackerman, studying at the University of Missouri, was in the midst of securing his own middle-class future, while Tina Medina, working as a receptionist, seemed at risk of losing the hard-earned middle-class status her family had attained. What separates these two families? In no small part, the government-backed benefit and policy support structures and quantities of employment capital available to the Ackermans and the Medinas through their jobs made all the difference in charting divergent futures for their children. These differences also explain why, even though skills seem similar, the Ackermans' family income is greater and why their economic and retirement security is far more robust. Access to wealth-building escalators on the job can mean the difference between stability and instability, between moving ahead and losing ground.

It should not matter that the Ackermans are white and the Medinas are African American. Nevertheless race is a crucial factor putting the children of these two families, Peter and Tina, on their differing trajectories. Innate ability, character differences, and superior values play little role in their future prospects, despite the readiness of many commentators to attribute racial differences in mobility and educational achievement to such factors. Peter and Tina were very different people, with their own interests and passions, but both were equally determined to get ahead in life. But their parents' jobs and benefit structures, and the sort of wealth accumulation and economic status those jobs enabled, largely dictated their paths. In the United States today, access to the best jobs with benefits diverges sharply based on race.

Similarly educated, with similar skills and similar ambitions, the Ackermans and the Medinas were nevertheless divided by vast differences in wealth accumulation, retirement security, and life chances. The Ackermans help illustrate the kinds of work situations that provide employment capital and thereby enable opportunity and mobility; the Medinas suggest what is missing in work situations that make well-being more contingent and fragile. Today, fewer and fewer families have access to opportunities like those the Ackermans enjoyed. And they and the Medinas both are part of a larger trend in the United States toward employers and corporations hollowing out good, middle-income jobs and hence the middle class.

THE EMPLOYMENT LANDSCAPE HAS CHANGED DRAMATICALLY in the United States. In 1970, General Motors (GM) employed 550,000 workers. It was the largest private employer in the United States, paying good salaries and offering benefits similar in fundamental ways to those the Ackermans enjoyed. Nearly half a century later, a corporate-driven globalizing economy has produced a major employment transformation. In 2015, Walmart was the largest American employer, with over 1.3 million workers at predominantly low-paying, low-benefit jobs—jobs more like the Medinas'. According to one estimate, Walmart's low-wage workers cost US taxpayers an estimated $6.2 billion in public assistance—including food stamps, Medicaid, and subsidized housing—because their wages are so low that they qualify for those safety net programs.[6] Walmart's average salaries are under $10 an hour; GM's starting wage in 1970 was the equivalent of $23.58 in 2015 dollars. The transformation from GM to Walmart captures the grand sweep of America's changing job landscape over recent decades.

National data confirm how rapidly the United States is moving in this direction—toward fewer jobs like the Ackermans' and more like the Medinas'. The Bureau of Labor Statistics (BLS) has accurately projected job growth in the United States for over twenty years. The long-term trend to-

TABLE 3.1 Occupations with Most Job Growth

1998–2008	2012–2022
Systems Analysis	Personal Care Aides
Retail Sales	Registered Nurses
Cashiers	Retail Salespersons
Managers and Executives	Home Health Aides
Truck Drivers	Food Preparation and Servers
Office Clerks	Nursing Assistants
Registered Nurses	Secretaries, Admin. Assistants
Computer Support Specialists	Customer Service
Home Health Aides	Janitors, Cleaners
Teacher Assistants	Construction Laborers

ward lower-paying and less-skilled service jobs was already plainly evident as we embarked on our initial family interviews in 1998. According to BLS data, those occupations with the largest growth between 1998 and 2008 were already tilting toward jobs that required less education and skill and paid people a lower return on their work. The BLS job-growth projections for 2012 to 2022, shown in Table 3.1, further extend the trend away from middle-income jobs. Employers need fewer executive-functioning skills, while low-wage jobs without career ladders leading to more responsibility and better pay are rising.[7]

This sweeping occupational shift away from middle-income jobs is part of a larger economic transformation since the early 1970s as the United States, like the world's other most developed nations, has positioned itself in the global economy. Industrial sectors have shrunk inexorably in size and economic impact, while service and health sectors have become the prime engines of increased economic output and employment expansion. The rate of service-sector expansion and especially the return from work on newly created service jobs are closely related to wage inequality. Women and workers of color have been greatly impacted by this transition because their employment is disproportionately concentrated in the service sector. Scholars, commentators, and politicians have debated ferociously about the fragile, anxious, squeezed, and declining middle class that has resulted from the hollowing out of mid-wage jobs. Arguing the causes for this transition, some point to a globalizing economy and deindustrialization, others to new technologies and machines, and still others to political factors such as liberalizing trade agreements, weakened labor unions, and a dwindling minimum wage. Regardless, the transformation of American work has had powerful effects on families like the ones we talked to—who were less concerned about the origins of these changes than with making their way through this altered landscape. The real pain and deeper struggles families face as a result of work and pay transformations, and the reasons behind them, may reverberate in national elections as politicians pander to the public and the media by shifting the conversation to unfair trade, imports, lost jobs, and immigration.[8]

The Great Recession sped up the transformation of American employment while starkly revealing longer-term effects on unemployment and underemployment, lower labor force participation, diminished work hours, and lower hourly wages. Not simply collateral damage associated with episodic economic downturns, these changes have become baked into the new economy. The devastating result of this changing employment landscape has been a lower standard of living for most families in the United States. In the immediate shock of the recession, 8.4 million people lost work, and median income for working-age families dropped by a tenth from where it had been in the first years of the new century. The economy contracted by 5.1 percent. One in seven Americans was living in poverty, and one in five children was growing up in a household below the poverty line. And these aggregate numbers mask how the imploding economy more harshly devastated young families, those without college degrees, and families of color. Although the Great Recession officially ended in June 2009, many of the families we interviewed between 2010 and 2012 continued to experience its impact profoundly. In 2013, median household income was $52,250, 8.0 percent lower than in 2007, the year before the recession began, and 8.2 percent lower than the 1999 peak.[9]

Accelerating an employment transformation already in the making, the Great Recession produced a "new normal" in which more and more Americans find themselves in the position of the Medinas. By 2014, the nation's payrolls had rebounded to pre-2006 highs, but the working-age population had also grown over those years, making the rebound less impressive. Moreover, the vast majority of job losses during the recession were in middle-income occupations, which have largely been replaced by lower-wage jobs. Mid-wage occupations (those paying between $13.83 and $21.13 per hour) made up about 60 percent of the job losses during the recession. But those mid-wage jobs have made up just 27 percent of the jobs gained during the recovery. As of mid-2014, total employment in the relatively high-paying construction and manufacturing sectors was down more than 3 million as compared to before the recession. Other sectors of the economy, such as food preparation, temp work, and retail sales, have added 3 million jobs. Average hourly pay of food and sales workers ranges from $12 to $16. These lower-wage jobs, with no or meager benefits, have continued to reshape the economy since the recession. In contrast, the lost jobs in manufacturing and construction paid between $24 and $27 and often had health, family, and retirement benefits.[10]

The declining share of middle-income jobs since the 1970s reflects a polarizing labor market that puts little value on routine work but offers ever-bigger rewards to those with specialized knowledge and skills. From the end of World War II to 1973, employers shared huge gains in productivity somewhat equitably, resulting in the doubling of American living standards; since the early 1970s, however, they have uncoupled the productivity-to-wages nexus. Between 1979 and 2013, productivity grew 64.9 percent, while annual inflation-adjusted income for 80 percent of the workforce grew just 16 percent. This loss of shared prosperity for the many did not affect the few as they commandeered greater incomes at the top of the ladder—the top 1 percent gained 174 percent, and the next 19 percent of highest incomes flourished by 58 percent. Productivity grew eight times faster than typical worker paychecks, and living standards for most workers stagnated.[11]

Family strategies to compensate for blocked growth in living standards include working more hours and deferring retirement, working more than one job, combining regular jobs with self-employment, and sending additional family members into the paid workforce. As a result, families have increased their on-the-job working hours significantly since 1970, working 14.5 percent more hours each week, or eleven additional weeks each year, in an effort to keep pace.[12] The increased work time is greater in families with lower-paying jobs. The additional hours come largely from people working more than one job and from women entering the paid workforce. Indeed, the number of family members working has grown significantly. From 1970 until the Great Recession, the average number of workers per family rose to 1.45 from 1.16. This increase is even more substantial considering the average family size has decreased by 25 percent since 1970. More members of smaller families spent more time working. Such an increase in family work hours can erode the quality of family life, even if family incomes keep pace.

The working experience of the Ackermans and Medinas illustrates a larger transformation in America's employment landscape, away from middle-class jobs and jobs with significant benefits toward low-paying jobs with few benefits, accelerated by the Great Recession. The postrecession job recovery has centered on stagnating lower wages and few benefits. Moreover, the Ackermans enjoy the protection of robust workplace benefits that endow their family's future but are largely unavailable to the Medinas. Precisely these sorts of benefits are becoming rarer and rarer as employers shift the employment landscape and it becomes polarized. The Ackermans' and Medinas' stories layer in racial wage differences as well. Whites disproportionately hold the kinds of quality, wealth-escalating job benefits so crucial to the Ackermans' well-being.

SINCE THE RECESSION, WAGES HAVE STAGNATED, WITH WORKers of color especially poorly off. In 2013, the median weekly earnings for a full-time worker were $797. This is a scant $2 more than ten years earlier. Furthermore, earnings differ sharply depending on race and ethnicity, with Hispanics and African Americans earning considerably less than whites and Asians. In 2013, median weekly earnings for full-time wage and salary workers were $578 for Hispanics and $629 for African Americans, compared with $802 for whites and $942 for Asians.[13] African American workers received seventy-eight cents and Hispanics seventy-two cents for each dollar paid to white workers. Although some of this distance results from differing education, skills, and occupations, the distance narrowed but significant gaps remained even within similar occupations. For example, among professionals working full-time, African Americans' salaries are 85 percent of whites'.

Pay differences by race readily convert to income and wealth inequality. But there is more to the story. Furthermore, as the Ackermans' story suggests, looking at wages alone can lead us to underestimate the magnitude and significance of income and wealth inequality. Several important items in Allison Ackerman's total compensation package are hidden when we examine her earnings. Specifically, her employer contributed about $5,100 annually to her defined contribution retirement account; it paid about $5,500 toward the cost of her family's health insurance; and critically, it paid her son's $20,000 tuition. Allison's paycheck masks approximately $30,600 worth of benefits. While the Ackermans are liable for taxes on the tuition benefit, the health-care benefit is not taxed, and taxes on the retirement account are deferred. Allison's actual paycheck—her official earnings—severely underestimates the actual resources and protections her job provides. The related tax exemptions and deferrals also amount to extensive and concealed public subsidies. Paid sick leave, vacation and personal days, disability insurance, and stable work are further benefits, harder to quantify but indispensable to economic security.

We have seen how the kinds of quality jobs held by the Ackerman family are enormously valuable, increasingly rare, and harder to access for nonwhite workers. Many efforts to combat inequality have simply focused on removing barriers in education and employment that keep nonwhite workers from jobs with higher incomes and hearty benefits. Much progress has been made in legislation and employment practices and policies, such as Title VII of the Civil Rights Act of 1964, prohibiting employment discrimination based on race, color, religion, sex, or national origin; the Equal Pay Act of 1963; Titles I and V of the Americans with Disabilities Act of 1990; and the Civil Rights Act of 1991, providing damages in cases of intentional employment discrimination. In addition, employers offering retirement accounts must market them to all eligible workers, not just to top pay grades or management. Liberals have traditionally held that removing barriers to opportunity is the silver-bullet answer to eliminating inequality, and the passage of major employment and civil rights laws has eliminated much formalized and explicit discrimination. Yet a growing body of research has begun to push past this orthodoxy and proposes that, as important as removing obstacles to opportunity may be, we need to dig deeper.[14]

The view that individuals have difficulty finding and keeping decent, mid-wage work due to inadequate social skills and a lack of job preparation and competence underpins a plethora of work-training programs. Addressing this opportunity obstacle is critical; yet it puts the onus of mobility entirely on individual workers. Many questions remain unaddressed, and I will follow up on just one: the financial gain of better jobs for blacks and whites. The very robust educational emphasis on inequality assumes that gaps will narrow considerably as we close in on college-completion parity. The tremendous gain in lifetime earnings due to attainment of a college degree over a high school diploma ($1 million), just some college ($700,000), or an associate's degree ($500,000) is well documented, impressive, and important for individual mobility and better job security. While removing obstacles to college completion, whatever they may be, is crucial, we also need to ask whether college degrees result in considerably more financial gain for whites than blacks.[15]

Even when people of color get higher-earning jobs, because they are less likely to have good benefits, their paychecks do not translate into similar financial gain as for whites. Liberal and mainstream economic theory assumes that equal opportunity is the path to parity. This ignores the fact that equal achievements on the job and fatter paychecks yield unequal wealth rewards for whites and African Americans. Not surprisingly, increases in income are a major source of wealth accumulation for many US families. However, research by the Institute on Assets and Social Policy shows that similar income gains for whites and African Americans have a very different impact on wealth accumulation. Every $1 increase in average income over a twenty-five-year period converted to $5.19 wealth for white households but added only sixty-nine cents of wealth for African American households. The dramatic difference in wealth accumulation from similar income gains has its roots in long-standing patterns of discrimination in hiring, training, promoting, and granting access to benefits that have made it much harder for African Americans to save and build assets. Furthermore, broader family networks entailing mutual obligations tip priorities toward financially helping others at the expense of their own savings. As previously described, black workers predominate in administrative, support, and food services, which are least likely to have employer-based retirement plans and other benefits due to discriminatory factors such as occupational segregation that concentrates them into jobs offering lesser packages. As a result, wealth in black families tends to hover around what is needed to cover emergency savings, while wealth in white families far exceeds the emergency threshold, allowing them to save or invest additional dollars of income more readily.[16]

The statistics cited above about divergent wealth gains from rising incomes compare change in median wealth over twenty-five years for typical white and black households. Yet we already know that the average white family starts out with abundantly more wealth and a significantly higher income than the average black family. When whites and African Americans start off on a footing with similar wealth portfolios, gaps in wealth gains from similar rising income narrow considerably.

One of the most widely watched indicators of an economy's health is the unemployment rate. Unemployment is also the most common cause of pressure on family finances, stress in family relationships, and changes in family members' life trajectories. Prior to the Great Recession, the US unemployment rate had been at or below 5 percent for the previous two and a half years. It peaked at 10.0 percent in October 2009. At the end of 2014, official unemployment was at 5.8 percent, but that figure climbed to 11.5 percent once part-time workers who wanted full-time work and those marginally attached to the labor force were added in. In addition these figures mask the pervasive reality of unemployment over the long run: over a twelve-year period (1998–2010), two in five families had a working member who experienced at least one spell of unemployment.[17]

All families do not experience employment disruptions similarly. Unemployment is a more frequent and prolonged event for African Americans than it is for whites. The national unemployment rate in 2013 for African American workers was double what it was for whites—13.1 percent for African Americans and 6.5 percent for whites—and the Hispanic rate was 9.1 percent.[18] The same phenomenon also appears in longitudinal national data. Between 1999 and 2012, close to half of African American families (46 percent) experienced a period of unemployment, while just over one-third of white families did (34.6 percent).[19] For African Americans, unemployment spells are more frequent, last longer, and end with new work at lower pay. African Americans, as well as Hispanics and immigrants, tend to be employed in sectors very sensitive to business cycles. When the general economy is doing poorly, populations concentrated in those sectors feel the effects more quickly and find that these effects last longer. The notion that working people of color are the last to be hired in a good economy and the first to be laid off when there's a downturn carries much wisdom and empirical verification. Blacks with more precarious labor force attachments are indeed the last people to be hired as employers need more workers and are in fact disproportionately more likely to lose their jobs during slowdowns and recessions as the business cycle weakens.[20]

Because wages, benefits, and the likelihood of unemployment vary dramatically according to occupation and economic sector, occupational segregation is an important factor in why workers of color fare more poorly than whites. After taking educational attainment into account, seven out of every eight US occupations can be classified as racially segregated, according to one of the better studies of the issue. This study found that black men, for example, are represented proportionally to their share of the overall working population in only 13 percent of occupations. Black men are underrepresented in high-paying occupations and overrepresented in those with low wages. The average earnings of occupations in which black men are overrepresented is $37,005, compared with $50,333 in occupations in which they are underrepresented. Neither difference in skills nor

in occupational interests fully explains occupational segregation, the study concluded, suggesting that the phenomenon
is embedded in historic employment patterns.[21]

Sociologists often explain historic employment patterns
as resulting from economic restructuring, focusing on blacks'
economic fortunes and emphasizing the rise and fall of the
industrial economy and what industries and jobs they worked
in. Historic employment patterns result partially from the
shifting job structure as we moved from an industrial to a
service economy. Data from the 1940s onward also suggest
that political and institutional factors—the labor, civil rights,
and women's movements, government policies, unionization
efforts, and public-employment patterns—have significantly
influenced paycheck inequities. Additional nonmarket factors like racial discrimination have long shaped black economic fortunes powerfully. This discriminatory employment
pattern is especially evident in the management and professional occupations.[22]

Despite laws, labor market discrimination persists as a
major mechanism that maintains and extends occupational
segregation. Some like to think that bias and discrimination
are things of the past and play no part in inequality today,
but research shows otherwise. In one experiment, researchers responded to help-wanted ads in two cities with resumes
bearing either African American– or white-sounding names,
then tracked the number of callbacks each resume received
for job interviews. They sent out nearly 5,000 resumes for
positions ranging from cashier and clerical worker to office
and sales manager. Half of the applicants had names "remarkably common" among African Americans; the other

half had white-sounding names, such as Emily Walsh or Greg Baker. All other qualifications listed on the resumes—work history, skills, and experience—were equivalent; the race-identifying names were the sole difference. The results indicated large racial differences in callback rates. Job applicants with African American names needed to send 50 percent more resumes to receive a callback, a statistically very significant gap. The researchers concluded that implicit bias among employers continues to shape employment prospects for whites and blacks.[23]

Other rigorous research examining the impact of incarceration on subsequent employment opportunities demonstrates the role played by the intersection of race and criminal justice. Black applicants with criminal records labor under a double burden—and given the racial inequities in the criminal justice system, black applicants are more likely to have such records. White men with criminal records had more positive responses to job applications than black men without them.[24] Criminal records have a significant negative impact on job prospects for all applicants, reducing the likelihood of a callback or job offer by nearly 50 percent. However, the negative effect of a criminal conviction is substantially larger for blacks than for whites. This finding suggests that contemporary employment discrimination alone has an effect equivalent to a criminal conviction for black job seekers.[25]

The favoritism that white workers show toward other whites—especially in their search for good jobs that pay a living wage and that provide benefits—also reproduces racial inequality and occupational segregation. Want ads, websites, and public announcements are formal venues for job seekers, and most think that people find employment through them. A study of informal mechanisms in the workplace found that throughout their lives the majority of whites utilized social networks to learn about openings and find jobs, thereby protecting themselves from competition in the job market. Three-quarters of working men and 60 percent of working women said their social networks had given them a leg up in learning about a job opening and getting hired. Searching job ads played a minor part. This study built upon earlier research on social networks in employment, which showed that African Americans are less likely to obtain quality leads to employment from their networks relative to similarly situated whites.[26] The power of informal social networks in helping people find jobs perpetuates existing racial inequity in the workplace.

Much has been accomplished in the years since major civil rights legislation of the 1960s opened new educational and occupational opportunities to African Americans, women, and others. African Americans have made tremendous strides in educational attainment and job performance, reaching the highest positions in virtually every occupation in America. Yet occupational segregation and labor market discrimination remain high, and they reproduce racial inequality in income and wealth. Without access for all to secure jobs that provide employment capital and wealth escalators, toxic inequality will continue to grow and to divide.

AFTER A LIFETIME OF WORK, WE ALL HOPE TO RETIRE SECURELY, comfortably, and with dignity. The security or insecurity of retirement depends not only on the cumulative earnings of one's working life but also on one's access to an employer-based pension or retirement savings plan. As the employment landscape renders working lives more unstable and fragmented, the goal of retirement becomes more problematic and contingent. Our interviews strongly suggest that retirement is becoming more and more an exclusively upper-middle-class notion. Many families we spoke to scoffed at the idea of retirement, telling us they would work until they could no longer do so, not until they choose not to. The Wards were one of these families.

Aaron and Felicia Ward, fifty-one and forty-nine, respectively, when we met with them in 2011, both worked most of their adult lives while sending several of their children to college. Felicia had stopped working when she was diagnosed with lupus. Aaron, a self-employed carpenter, also worked construction to supplement his income when his own business slowed down. The couple raised and legally adopted two of Felicia's nieces because the girls' biological mother was on drugs and could not care for them. The Wards contributed regularly to their church and to the Lupus Foundation, and they helped out other family members financially.

As we talked in their home in the Dorchester section of Boston, the atmosphere was friendly and spiced with self-deprecating yet enlightening humor. Toward the end of our conversation, we turned to their retirement plans. I asked if they had any retirement accounts or money put aside. "No," Aaron jested, "I got some bottles downstairs. Cans and bottles. That's our retirement. Bottles and cans. That's our retirement; just stack them up in the basement." I asked if they were thinking about when they might retire. Aaron jumped in, "What's that [retirement]? You mean dying? Expiring?" Felicia added that she was already basically retired because she was not supposed to go back to work due to her illness. Aaron said, "I doubt if I'll ever retire. I'll have to hit the lottery in order to retire."

The African American Ward family—joking about redeeming bottles stored in their basement and hoping their lottery number came up—presented a stark contrast to the white Ackerman family, with its $350,000 in retirement savings. But the dramatic differences in the two families' retirement security did not result from individual behaviors and characteristics, like risk taking, deferring gratification, thrift, or superior financial decision making. Rather, they were the result of the jobs the Wards and the Ackermans had worked. Allison Ackerman had the good fortune to work in an economic sector that offered generous savings benefits at an institution that mandated and then matched contributions to a retirement account. The two families' stories illustrate how deep structures shape well-being and create inequality along economic and racial lines. Differing work situations and differential access to employer-based benefits placed the Ackermans and Wards on two separate wealth-accumulation paths and shaped the futures they could contemplate for themselves. The ability to save for retirement is another crucial manifestation of the racial wealth gap and another important aspect of toxic inequality.

The federal Social Security program (1935) is the foundation of the retirement system in the United States, and from the very start it mirrored and locked in racial and gender inequalities that already existed in the working world. Coverage was far from universal because Congress excluded agricultural and domestic workers, affecting African Americans in the South the most, as two-thirds of them worked on farms or in domestic service. Thus the system started by including about half of the workforce. Those seniors today receiving Social Security far surpass the percentage receiving income from any other source. The amount a family is eligible to draw upon in retirement depends on what its members put in, which in turn depends on how long they worked and how stably, their pay levels, and whether the system included their occupation. Social Security provides widespread but not universal coverage; as of 2010, 14.4 percent of persons aged sixty-five or older were not receiving income from Social Security as they lacked sufficient paid and reported work histories to gain coverage. Most were late-arriving immigrants, infrequent workers, and noncovered workers. This excluded group was disproportionately female, Hispanic, less educated, newly arrived in the United States, and either never married or widowed.

Social Security provides slightly more than half (52.3 percent) of the income that sustains older couples and nearly three-quarters (73.8 percent) of the income that sustains older individuals. Over one in five couples and nearly half of single seniors rely on Social Security for the huge bulk—at least 90 percent—of their incomes. Nearly a third (31.5 percent) of African American single seniors rely entirely on Social Security for their income. Among Latino

single seniors, 37.3 percent get all of their income from Social Security, whereas 25.5 percent of single Asian seniors
depend entirely upon Social Security.[27]

Among typical recipients, benefits are modest: the median
figure is $24,346 annually for married couples and $14,207 for
singles. The figures suggest how Social Security was intended
to provide only a foundation for retirement, not to fully resource the senior years after a lifetime of work. The legislation was part of President Franklin D. Roosevelt's New Deal,
and several times he publicly stated that workplace-based
retirement plans and personal savings would supplement Social Security payments. The program aimed fundamentally to
prevent impoverishment among the elderly who had worked
most of their lives or their spouses or children. But although
Social Security provides a modest source of economic security
for seniors, employer plans and other savings fall far short of
making this economic security truly robust. On average, only
about half of the American workforce is enrolled in a pension
plan. Although 57 percent of wage and salary employees aged
twenty-five to sixty-four work for an employer that sponsors
a retirement plan, only 48 percent actually participate in it.
Access varies considerably depending on race. Some 62 percent of white workers have access to an employer-provided
retirement plan, while only 54 percent of black and Asian
employees do. Latinos fare even worse, with only 38 percent
employed in firms that offer a retirement plan.[28]

Increasingly, employers are offering less reliable and risk-
ier retirement plans. Defined benefit plans, which guarantee
workers a specific income on retirement (often a percentage
of their salary in their last years at work), are giving way to

defined contribution plans, where the employee owns an account, like a 401(k). Pension coverage was never universal, but today less than half of workers (45 percent) have any type of pension provided by their employer.[29] Whereas 62 percent of workers enrolled in a single retirement plan in 1983 had a defined benefit pension, by 2013, 71 percent of those enrolled in a single plan had defined contribution plans like 401(k)s. (Some workers—13 percent in 2013—held both types of plans.[30]) The transition from defined benefits to defined contributions significantly shifts the risk and financial burden of saving for retirement from employers to individual workers. Whereas defined benefit plans provide participants with steady payouts for as long as they live, defined contribution plans generally allow working people to take money out as needed or to purchase an annuity. This mean that retirees have to decide how much to draw upon during each year of their retirement. They face the risk of spending too quickly and outliving their resources or spending too conservatively, depriving themselves of necessities, and dying with money to spare.

Racial disparities in plan access are especially pronounced in the private sector. African Americans, Asians, and Latinos are respectively 15, 13, and 42 percent less likely than whites to have access to a job-based retirement plan in the private sector. (In the public sector, differences remain but are smaller.) Households of color lag behind white households in coverage by defined benefit pensions that guarantee lifetime retirement income; they are only two-thirds as likely as whites to hold such pensions. And when it comes to liquid retirement savings from defined contribution plans and other vehicles, the racial gap is growing wider. In 2013, white families had seven times more in retirement savings than African American families and eleven times more than Hispanic families. In 1989, white families had $25,000 more than African American and Hispanic families, and this disparity quadrupled to $100,000 in 2013. This gap is becoming more consequential as liquid retirement savings vehicles like 401(k)s replace traditional defined benefit pension plans.[31]

Generally, workers who enjoy higher earnings are likely to obtain more benefits. But access to benefits is also strongly associated with race; sociodemographic differences, employment context, occupation, and earnings alone cannot account for the entire gap in access to benefits between whites and Latinos and between whites and African Americans.[32] Controlling for individual characteristics, African Americans' and Latinos' relative odds of obtaining benefits from employment are substantially lower than those of whites. Access to workplace-based benefits maps onto occupational segregation. African Americans, Asians, and particularly Latinos are less likely than whites to be employed in industries and occupations that provide high wages and workplace benefits, including retirement benefits.

These findings underscore the cumulative nature of economic and racial inequality and indicate rather strongly that measurements based only on earnings underestimate the actual magnitude of economic and racial disparity produced in the labor market.

Even for families like the Wards who are attempting to save for retirement, urgent necessities, unforeseen crises, and conflicting priorities can confound the best of intentions. Unemployment is more widespread, frequent, and longer lasting among workers of color. Necessity often requires tapping retirement accounts for daily needs, to pay bills, or to keep foreclosure or eviction at bay. Our interviews suggested, and national data confirm, that many American families, especially African Americans and Hispanics, treat retirement accounts as flexible, emergency cash reserves rather than as long-term savings vehicles. These employer-based accounts are often the only pots of money available to them in times of need. While part of the attraction of these assets for many people is their relative liquidity, these plans were not meant to function as lifeboats during periods of national economic hardship. When they are the only resources available, the result is a brutal choice between meeting expenses today and funding a secure retirement for tomorrow.

African Americans and Hispanics are especially likely to confront this choice. A 2012 survey of retirement plans found that about six in ten African Americans and Hispanics who lost their jobs because of layoffs or for other reasons cashed out their retirement savings plans entirely, compared to fewer than four in ten whites and Asian Americans.[33] African Americans were also more than four times as likely as whites to take a hardship withdrawal from their retirement savings plans. Even when other contributing factors such as salary and age are held constant, African Americans are 276 percent and Hispanics are 47 percent more likely than whites to take hardship withdrawals for their immediate and extended families.[34]

Families of color often have different kinship obligations than white families. One key difference is the relative capacity for and priority of helping family members in times of need in relation to saving for retirement. In a survey of 19,000 employees at sixty of America's largest corporations, 36 percent of African American employees and 38 percent of Hispanics (compared with 24 percent of whites and 21 percent of Asian Americans) said that they had more pressing financial priorities and did not prioritize saving for retirement. Those other priorities, as our family interviews revealed, often included helping members in the larger familial network. In our interviews, white families disclosed a broad pattern of *receiving* financial assistance from other family members in times of need, perhaps mitigating the need to borrow, load expenses onto credit cards, or drain money from accounts dedicated to retirement or college. In contrast, successful African American families in particular were called upon far more often than their white counterparts to *provide* help to kin. We heard this time and time again. It is enormously beneficial to have extended family members who are financially more successful, especially if they are willing to help in times of need or to assist in taking advantage of an opportunity. Our family interviews mirror large survey data showing that college-educated black households provided financial support to their parents three times more often compared to white college-educated households.[35] Extended family members with few resources are simply not in a position to help, which is often the case for blacks. Felicia Ward's personal experience is exemplary. She told us, "I can't go to my family for nothing as far as help financially, because they got their own problems."

THE ACKERMANS, THE MEDINAS, AND THE WARDS LIVE VERY different lives, enjoy very different degrees of economic security, and see very different futures for themselves and their young adult children. Their lives suggest the vast inequities that result when only some people have secure jobs in stable economic sectors with ample benefits, including employer-matched retirement accounts and college tuition assistance, and others, disproportionately people of color, have lower-paying work in sectors more susceptible to business cycles, in jobs providing few benefits, little access to retirement accounts, and no help in making college more affordable. The great differences in family wealth and well-being that result from employment are a crucial source of toxic inequality.

New York Times columnist David Brooks asks three questions that he suggests account for success or failure in life. Are you living for short-term pleasure or long-term good? Are you living for yourself or for your children? Do you have the freedom of self-control, or are you in bondage to your desires?[36] Whether or not one thinks these are the right questions to ask, one thing is abundantly clear: the Ackermans and Medinas live their lives by the same answers, but without substantial changes to our contemporary employment landscape, the worlds of Peter Ackerman and Tina Medina will only grow further apart.

As important as it is, transforming the employment landscape is not the only change needed. In our 1998 conversation, Kendrick Johnson, whom we met in Chapter 1, posed a very different question about success in life. As a highly successful professional, he described driving to work every day through affluent suburbs and asking himself the same question: "I'm driving to work from Orange County, Laguna, Newport, and I'm looking at these houses and saying, 'What are these people doing for a living, and how come I'm not doing it?'" In Chapter 4 we meet individuals who live in those kinds of communities, and we answer Kendrick's question about what those families have that his doesn't: an inheritance.

=4=

THE INHERITANCE ADVANTAGE

"Scary," Blake Mills mused aloud, pondering the amount of money he had inherited and how much it had transformed his family's prospects. Blake acknowledged that inheritance was the reason he and his wife owned a home in an upscale beachside community. It had enabled him to absorb a pay cut, allowed his wife to choose to move from paid work to watching over their sons, and pushed their boys into high-quality schools.

Money passed from generation to generation can be measured in dollars easily enough, but its enormous impact in transforming lives is harder to quantify. Inherited assets give those who receive them a huge head start in life and provide incalculable, unearned advantages; inheritance belies the idea that people enjoy generally equal opportunities and rise or fall on merit alone. Scariest of all, America's history of racial exclusion and vast inequities in wealth accumulation collide most dramatically in inheritance.

Inheritances and other gifts—small and large—are unquestionably important for their recipients, allowing them to build wealth, affording protection from emergencies, and providing economic security. Some inherited monies are saved or invested right away, immediately expanding family wealth. Usually, however, the wealth gains happen over a longer period. Time and again, our interviews revealed families using inherited money to pay for their children's education or as a down payment on a home, investments that pay off over time. For instance, sixty-seven of the ninety-four home-owning families we spoke with between 2010 and 2012 had received family financial assistance in making the down payments on their homes. Gifts can also help families absorb unexpected shocks, like car-repair or medical bills, and pay expenses after the loss of a job or a reduction in hours. These cash transfers don't produce a rising balance in a savings account or otherwise increase a family's wealth in the short term; yet the availability of such protective resources can forestall hardship, with long-term implications for family stability and wealth. Inherited wealth can completely alter a family's trajectory, as the story of the Clark family shows.

THE CLARKS LIVED IN ONE OF ST. LOUIS's MOST COVETED suburbs. Carline Clark worked part-time as an accountant, and her husband had left social work a few years before to work for a not-for-profit. Their spacious house was valued at over $750,000 when we spoke with them in 2010, and their children attended excellent, exclusive schools. Something seemed out of place. With a combined income of $70,000, the family should not have been able to afford such an expensive home in an upper-income community or such costly private school tuition.

In fact they couldn't afford these things based on their income alone. Rather, a large inheritance had catapulted the Clarks' wealth to well over $1 million, and they expected to receive plenty more from their parents in the future. Although they thought of themselves as part of the middle class, their wealth in fact situated them close to the richest 5 percent of Americans. And like many wealthy families, they were not self-made. Inheritance was the source of their success and status. Their $70,000 family income was larger than most, placing them solidly in the middle class and providing resources most working-class or impoverished families struggle to attain. But their inherited wealth gave them multiple, concrete opportunities and advantages they would not otherwise have. The Clarks' wealth allowed them to live in a home and community beyond the means of their income; it enabled one of their children to overcome learning difficulties; it paid for private schooling and college tuition; and it allowed them not to worry about retirement. They served as a living example of wealth's power to transform lives and sustain advantages, to provide near-immunity against failure, and to supply multiple second chances.

In 2010 we asked Carline, "Do you feel a sense of economic security?" Her tone became terse and defensive. "Yes," she replied, because "my parents have money." Twelve years earlier she was more self-assured in her response to the same question. Back then, she readily admitted that, even though she and her husband did not have huge incomes, she felt that her family was very comfortably situated, with money available anytime they needed it. Perhaps her change in tone revealed a new sensitivity to the way the Great Recession was stripping away from those around her the rewards of years of hard work. Perhaps rhetoric critical of the "one percent" of richest Americans was beginning to make her more self-conscious regarding the advantages she enjoyed. Whatever the reason, in 2010 Carline appeared to recognize that life was different for her family than for others. Indeed, Carline understood well and articulated clearly the advantages that came with deep reservoirs of wealth. She said, for example, there was no question that she and her husband would not have had money to send their two children to an exclusive private school without the wealth they had inherited. Indeed, they could not have even considered it.

Inheritance had shaped the Clarks' lives for many years. Within the first year of their marriage, the Clarks bought their first home, a historic farmhouse, with money from Carline's parents and an inheritance from her grandmother. Their down payment totaled half of the purchase price—far higher than the national benchmark down payment for home purchases of between 5 and 15 percent. More than a quarter of home buyers (27 percent) put down 3 percent or less.[1] When we talked in 1998, Carline loved her own house but spoke disdainfully of her neighborhood—not all of the homes in this middle-class area were as nice as hers. She described her neighbors as young professionals on the way up, just starting out with smaller homes. Further separating them from their neighbors, the Clarks said they had no intention of "using the school district." Instead, Carline's parents would pay for private schools that three generations of the family had attended.

In 1998, Carline had already identified another neighborhood that she preferred. As she put it, she had her "eye on this area really close to our house but worlds away." Shortly after we spoke, the family moved, paying for the new house outright with $500,000 in cash given by her parents. In 2010, they estimated that the house's value had appreciated to $750,000. The Clarks had the means to cross neighborhood borders and move up in the world. Their passport was family wealth amassed in an era when it was almost impossible for African Americans to own homes, property, or businesses—to build wealth and pass its advantages along to subsequent generations. Carline's forebears had owned paper mills and a large tool-manufacturing company. They had also been trustees of a private subdivision of twenty-three houses built in the 1920s. Occupying slightly more than thirty-five acres in suburban St. Louis, it is still distinguished by its mature trees and large lots and the Old St. Louis splendor of its houses. Law and custom excluded African Americans and others; the St. Louis Real Estate Exchange's Uniform Restriction Agreement had declared, "It is to the mutual benefit and advantage of all of the parties . . . to preserve the character of said neighborhood . . . for persons of the Caucasian Race and to maintain the value of their respective properties . . . to restrict the use." Buyers had to agree not to "sell, convey, lease or rent to a negro or negroes."[2] Unlike Carline's white grandparents, African American families were denied the opportunity to build wealth through home equity in the subdivision. The legacies of residential segregation lived on in the wealth the Clarks now enjoyed.

In 2010, in addition to their home, that wealth included $100,000 in combined savings accounts in the names of the Clarks' two children. The accounts had been built through annual $13,000 gifts from Carline's mother, exactly the legal limit of tax-free gifts that can be given annually to individuals. (By 2014, that limit had increased to $14,000.) Carline's parents always tried to gift their children and grandchildren the maximum amount allowed by law, in part to reduce the size of their estate and their chances of having to pay taxes on it in the future. Furthermore, Carline said, "they don't need it, and we do." Although inheritance is often thought of as money passed to adult children in a single moment, upon the death of one or both parents, the family financial assistance that economists call "in vivo transfers" can make an enormous impact on the lives of recipients again and again. As Carline told us, her parents "recognize births, graduations, birthdays; or, if we need a new piece of furniture or appliance, they'll pay for that."

These gifts allowed the Clarks' children to flourish. Back in 1998, Carline was sure her son, Nicholas, had a learning disability, even though it was not medically diagnosed. His grandparents paid for his elite private school, a string of tutors and learning coaches, and after-school enrichment programs. When we spoke in 2010, we learned that Nicholas ultimately attended a small liberal arts college in Arkansas, and in addition to the $50,000 yearly tuition, his grandparents picked up room and board. The Clarks' sixteen-year-old daughter, Anne, was earning straight A's at her elite private school.

I asked Carline to imagine what her life might be like without her family's generous financial support. She pondered aloud the belt-tightening, loans, and mortgages it would take to afford the home in which she lived and the private schools her children attended. She would have had to go out and find a well-paying job, at the very least. It would put "real strain" on the family, she said, and ultimately she admitted that they "just couldn't swing it." Carline talked about how she would have seen herself differently as a mother had she worked full-time, how her husband would have needed to find different work, and how all this would have prompted great soul-searching. After considering a life without $1 million–plus inheritance, she declared, "It's unimaginable."

I also asked Carline what she thought the family's financial security would be like in ten years. She was not sure they would be in the same house but declared, "I think we'll be on sound financial ground, because that's just how we make decisions." Her response suggested that being on "sound financial ground" was a mark of good character and wise decision making. But as our interviews revealed, the choices available and the wisest course of action very often depend on a family's circumstances. What might be prudent for a wealthy family like the Clarks may be totally unimaginable for other families; similarly, what is rational for typical families who don't enjoy the advantage of inheritance may appear personally irresponsible to outsiders. Economic stress often confronts families with very difficult and wrenching choices.

Steve and Christa Barzak, for instance, were living separately in 2010—not because they no longer loved one another or could not get along but as a strategy for getting through financial misfortune. We first interviewed the couple in 1998 in the condo they owned in Heather Village in Los Angeles. Both were highly educated professionals, each a few credits short of advanced degrees. Working in telecommunications and creative media, Steve and Christa became mainstays of the black middle class that emerged once legal obstacles to education and employment were removed. Together they earned $122,000, although they remained saddled with $37,000 in student loans.[3] In 2007, however, just after refinancing the condo to pay for renovations that would make it a comfortable home for the long term, Steve was laid off. The couple had already put $20,000 into the condo's kitchen, but they needed to sell the property quickly because they could not afford to pay the mortgage while Steve was unemployed. Unable to get their asking price, they settled for a short sale, taking in less than the amount owed on the debt.

The Barzaks were able to borrow some money from family and friends so that their older daughter could stay in the private school she was attending. But they couldn't afford to keep the younger child in private school as well. Steve collected unemployment insurance, which helped to an extent. For the first year after the couple sold the condo, they rented a house and lived together, but when things got even harder economically, when Steve continued to have trouble finding work and the stress they had thought temporary proved enduring, they were forced to make more difficult decisions. The couple decided to live apart, because if Christa was living by herself, she could qualify for food stamps, cutting expenses while ensuring a more stable diet for the girls. Christa and the girls moved in with her brother, who did not ask for rent in their time of need. Some might condemn the couple for gaming the system by splitting up to gain food stamp eligibility or criticize them for denying their children a traditional two-parent household. But for the Barzaks, it was a sound financial decision that ensured the girls' well-being. Their story recalls that of Kendrick Johnson, the father who took a new job in a new city to support his family, even as his children moved with his wife to her mother's home in Florida. Although other personal considerations may well have been at play in the Johnsons' separation, Kendrick too made a decision in the best interests of his family. Lacking the advantages of inheritance, the Barzaks and the Johnsons made the choices their circumstances demanded.

Inherited wealth has bought the Clark family freedom from belt-tightening, loans, and mortgages, and it has granted them the freedom to work jobs they enjoy regardless of pay and to parent on their own terms. The point is not to begrudge their lifestyle or stir up class resentment. But it is important to see clearly and concretely the kinds of opportunities, privileges, and cumulative advantages that wealth confers, as well as the mind-set that makes such privilege seem natural. Opportunities are, in fact, integrally connected to resources, which is not to say that health, head starts for children, and a good life are exclusive domains of the wealthy. One cannot deny, however, how much the ecosystem of wealth and privilege improves the probability of attaining better life chances. Clearly, it has had a transformative impact on the Clark family.

THE QUESTION OF PRECISELY HOW MUCH FAMILY WEALTH IS
due to inheritance has long vexed economists, who have produced a huge range of estimates varying from as much as 80
percent to as little as 20 percent. A major difficulty in resolv-
ing the debate is the problematic distinction between inherited wealth and subsequent wealth accumulated from that
base. To take one notorious example, Donald Trump claims
to be a self-made billionaire many times over. Yet would his
wealth be so huge today if he had not inherited $200 million
from his real estate tycoon father? Similar questions apply
to the families we talked to. How do we think about a family's overall wealth when so much of it resides in equity in a
home, for which a parental gift served as the down payment?
Most economists would score the down payment as inheritance and describe any increase in the home's value as earnings from investment. Whether that's the right approach is
an open question. One recent study of the role of bequests in
wealth accumulation finds that inheritance accounts for 31
percent of net wealth.[4] Among the families we interviewed
with ample financial wealth, however, parental gifts and inheritance played an even more significant and decisive role.

In the end, precisely dividing out bequests from accumulated wealth is nearly impossible; nor is it a useful endeavor.
More important is acknowledging the crucial role inheritance
plays in opening opportunities, providing some families with
a healthy head start and ongoing financial support. Just as
critical, if not more so, is acknowledging how lack of parental wealth tethers most families to the vagaries of their paychecks. Earlier, we discussed asking Carline Clark to imagine
what her family's arc might have looked like absent bounti-

ful parental financial assistance. We might also ponder what might have happened if a family like Cindy Breslin's possessed the inherited resources the Clarks did—how Cindy's learning disability might have played out differently, how Keneysha's playing doctor might have led to her practicing medicine today. Although we will never know, there can be no doubting that inherited wealth makes a world of difference.

Just as clear are the large differences in inheritance by race and ethnicity. An examination of inheritance among blacks and whites suggests the powerful legacies of racial injustice in America. Inheritance is a linchpin of toxic inequality, for it is a phenomenon in which America's history of racism collides with the indisputable reality of inequality today. Historically, African Americans were systematically denied possibilities to build wealth, even as government policy delivered copious and bountiful wealth-building opportunities to some whites. Today, police brutality, mass incarceration, residential and occupational segregation, housing and employment discrimination, and voter suppression reveal the continuity of deep structures of racial injustice.

Racial injustice is both cause and consequence of African Americans' economic status. Past racial injustice was integral to preventing blacks from gaining economic security and wealth and is manifest to this day. For example, we can trace blacks' position in the contemporary employment landscape from slavery, through Jim Crow and their exclusion from the 1935 Social Security Act, to the high degree of ongoing occupational segregation that today maps onto lower pay, fewer benefits, and little wealth. African Americans confront these ongoing injustices with few protective wealth resources that might mitigate the severest consequences. Looking closely at inheritance helps to reveal how it will be impossible to overcome widening economic inequality without also dealing with the legacy of racial inequality and the widening racial wealth gap, or to overcome racial inequality without reversing the trend toward economic inequality.

Vast inequities in wealth mean that some households have greater access to financial assistance through an extended family's web of wealth. These families receive such assistance more frequently and in larger amounts. Over time, receiving large gifts and inheritances allows them to build substantially more wealth of their own. This reality emerges from a twenty-seven-year national, longitudinal study of income dynamics and from surveys covering shorter periods, as well as from our own family interviews in 1998 and 1999 and from 2010 to 2012.

The first thing to note is that large inheritance, in any form, is relatively infrequent. Only a minority of the population—white or black—is fortunate enough to amass wealth from parents. The Panel Survey on Income Dynamics (PSID), which followed the same households over more than a quarter century between 1984 and 2013, revealed how receiving financial transfers of $10,000 or more from extended family is relatively uncommon: only 35 percent of the working-age families followed by the survey had received such a transfer by 2011.[5] Most families, close to two-thirds of those tracked, received no large financial transfers from family members at any point over twenty-seven years.

Just over one-third of households nationally received family financial transfers over a generation, and there were stark racial disparities among the beneficiaries. The web of wealth that low-income and African American households can access is often severely curtailed because fewer relatives have built up significant financial resources of their own to draw on. White households were four and a half times more likely to receive inheritance or in vivo transfers (money passed between living parties) than African American households in the PSID study. Between 1984 and 2011, close to half of white households (46 percent) received some type of financial transfer, compared to only 10 percent of African American households. Single-year snapshots reveal similar disparities. An Urban Institute study showed that over a one-year period, both black and Hispanic families were five times less likely to receive large gifts and inheritances than white families. Another study showed that black families received substantially less in in vivo gifts and were substantially less likely to ever inherit than white families, and they inherited less money when they did inherit.[6]

This inheritance divide is a major driver of the growth in the racial wealth gap, because inherited wealth accumulates and compounds over time. Among the nearly half of white households receiving financial transfers, the median amount was $83,692. By contrast, among the one in ten African American households receiving a financial transfer, the median amount was $52,240.[7] Not only were African American households four times less likely to receive a financial transfer, but when they did, the median amount was $30,000 less than for white beneficiaries. Both disparities mean that African Americans have far less to invest in assets that might appreciate in value or in opportunities that might increase their future prosperity. It is the difference between grasping opportunities and having opportunities just beyond grasp.

If all the money inherited between generations among whites were somehow divvied up equally, each white family would amass $54,000. Meanwhile, every black and Hispanic family would inherit $9,130 and $5,160, respectively. We already know that not all families inherit; yet this sort of comparison shows that the ecology of privilege overwhelmingly grants the decisive advantage to whites.[8]

Numbers are fine, but does inheritance matter? Both the white and the black households that received extended family financial resources during the twenty-seven years of the PSID study were able to build significantly more wealth than those not inheriting. At the median, white inheritors amassed $282,000 more wealth during this period, compared to $72,000 among white noninheritors. African American beneficiaries also reported higher family wealth gains than African American households not receiving transfers: $20,000 versus $12,000 for noninheritors.[9] White households, however, saw greater wealth expansion for each dollar of family financial assistance received—most likely because African American households received fewer and smaller financial transfers and also because families of color give money to broad family networks more frequently than whites, as detailed later in this chapter.

Studies of shorter periods also show enormous differences by race and ethnicity in large gifts and inheritances, even after controlling for family economic and demographic factors like income, marital status, number of children, and age. One of the best reports found that, over a two-year period, 5.2 percent of white families were beneficiaries of large gifts or inheritances, compared to 1.3 percent of blacks and 1.4 percent of Hispanics.[10] As is wholly consistent with the longer, twenty-seven-year study, Hispanic and black families received considerably less in large gifts and inheritances than white families. Families of American-born blacks received an astounding $5,013 less in large gifts and inheritances, on average, than white families. Using a large, nationally representative sample (Survey of Income and Program Participation [SIPP]), the Urban Institute estimates that, over time, large gifts and inheritances account for 12 percent of the white-black wealth gap.

SIPP also reveals who *gives* and *receives* smaller amounts of financial support within family networks. Black families most frequently received support, followed by whites and then Hispanics. Close to one in six black families (15.9 percent) received financial support during the two-year period, compared to 10.4 percent for whites and 6.5 percent for Hispanics. Hispanic families were more likely to give support to their kin networks than whites and blacks, 14.2 percent compared to 8.8 percent for whites and 9.1 percent for blacks. Hispanics were more than five times as likely to support their parents as whites.

Despite receiving money more often, Hispanic immigrant and nonimmigrant and black families collected an average of $278 to $589 less per year in net support (receiving minus giving) than white families. This is because these minority groups received fewer dollars of support, and Hispanic families gave more in support than white families. These transfers among family networks tended to involve small amounts, measured in the tens and hundreds of dollars and generally consumed, not saved or invested. Our family interviews clearly indicated that these sorts of transfers are most often intended to cushion unforeseen and immediate economic hardships. They may also have long-term implications for family stability and asset building.[11]

Another way to understand the power and advantage of inheritance is to focus just on college-educated families with middle-class credentials. The data clearly demonstrate education's return on investment, especially the association of higher wealth with college and professional degrees compared to high school diplomas or less or partial college. But seen through a racial lens, recent data on the connection between education and wealth is both compelling and counterintuitive. College-educated whites increased their wealth significantly between 2007 and 2013 by $31,000, adjusted for inflation, while college-educated blacks lost nearly $20,000 in wealth during the same period.[12]

An investigation of the Institute on Assets and Social Policy (IASP) into the wealth-college association revealed one reason for this: the inheritance advantage. The team found that close to a third (32 percent) of white college-educated families received a large wealth transfer of $10,000 or more between 1989 and 2013. Fewer than one in ten (9 percent) college-educated black families received similar wealth transfers. Whites were 2.8 times more likely to receive such large gifts. Among college-educated whites receiving large transfers, half got more than $55,400, while the median figure for blacks was $36,000. The difference between the average figures for the two groups is far greater, $235,353 to $65,755.

Inheritance, of course, is not limited to large gifts or bequests. It also includes smaller financial transfers, usually made with a specific purpose in mind. For the first time, new data from PSID allow a detailed reckoning of this sort of family giving and receiving between generations. And IASP's study found that white college-educated families were significantly more likely to benefit from heftier financial support from parents in one year, 2012, receiving twice as much money as blacks, $1,000 compared to $500. Importantly, after becoming adults at eighteen, 64 percent of white college-educated individuals got parental help to pay for school compared to 34 percent of blacks. Even more notably, white parents contributed $73,500 on average to their children's education, compared to just over $16,000 for black college-educated parents. White parents also helped finance homes for their adult children more frequently than blacks, 12 versus 4 percent. And, again, the average amount of parental financial assistance for home ownership was stark, $66,700 compared to $6,400.[13] While white college graduates report significant assistance from their parents, black college graduates tell a *giving* story as opposed to a *receiving* story. Among blacks, 45 percent gave to parents in need compared to 16 percent of whites. In sum, inheritance and other transfers from family members were one crucial reason that college-educated white families gained wealth between 2007 and 2013, while college-educated black families lost wealth during the same period.

We witnessed a similar phenomenon in our family interviews. The parents we talked with were most likely to receive ongoing financial support from their families to assist them in raising young children, buying first homes or moving to larger ones, and preparing for college. More than three out of every four families we interviewed had received financial transfers from extended family. Indeed, the large majority of the white and black home owners we spoke to (sixty-seven of ninety-four) received family financial assistance to purchase their homes. Although the nationally representative surveys cited above offer a statistically more reliable guide to the scope, frequency, and amount of such transfers, our interviews nevertheless highlight the importance that parental support plays at key moments and suggest how much families rely on such support overall. As Carline Clark suggested, such support offers a private safety net and a launching pad for success. Knowing this money is available increases self-confidence and risk taking, enables pursuit of promising opportunities, and provides a sense of security all the while.

Our family interviews also revealed a great deal of context and texture regarding the circumstances that prompt families to give and receive money. In white families, especially the middle-class ones, resources flowed from older parents to adult children. One couple burst out laughing in a 1998 interview when I asked them if they financially helped their parents or other relatives. They explained that the question was simply ridiculous, because family resources streamed to them, and there was no need to help out parents, brothers, sisters, or other family. In contrast, resources flowed in a markedly more reciprocal pattern among working-class and minority families based on need and depending on the urgency of circumstances. Middle-class black families like the Johnsons and Wards, meanwhile, told us about the copious support they gave to extended family members in hard times or to pay for relatives' college. National surveys and our interviews both confirm that the movement of money within American families differs substantially depending on race and class and explains how inheritance and other financial transfers help to produce great divides in family wealth.

CARLINE CLARK'S FAMILY, HAVING INHERITED WELL OVER $1 million with more to come, is certainly not typical. Of the one in three white families fortunate enough to inherit, the median inheritance is much lower, around $84,000. But as the story of the Mills family suggests, an inheritance closer to this more typical figure can greatly impact a family's trajectory and transform lives.

We sat down with Blake and Andrea Mills in 1998 and 2010 in an upmarket section of Redondo Beach, once part of a 48,000-acre land grant from the Spanish government to the Dominguez family in 1822. During the Mexican-American War, US Marines laid siege to the Dominguez ranchero in 1848 and were driven back to their ships in the nearby harbor.[14] Today, it is one of Los Angeles's most highly coveted beach communities, a place where shoeless preppies sip espressos and gaze at the Pacific Ocean on gorgeous California days, most likely oblivious of the history of the ground they stand on. The story of this place, of how property was titled and transferred through land grants, wars, seizures, and court battles between feuding pioneer families, then subdivided, sold to aviation industry workers during World War II, and eventually gentrified—this is the sweeping arc of history in its repeated interactions with individual families' circumstances.

Much as King Charles III of Spain bequeathed land rights to a chosen elite, Blake's parents anchored his family in Redondo

Beach with a large gift. Blake and Andrea in all probability could not have afforded to purchase their home on their own, even with their very good family income of $97,000. Rather, inheritance placed them and their two sons in one of California's best-resourced, most educationally rich school districts.

In the early 1990s Blake and Andrea were living in a South Bay apartment in an area they liked a lot. Blake's father proposed that they buy a place in Redondo Beach together. Blake agreed, and father and son became co-owners of a townhouse. Eventually Blake's father took himself off the deed, giving Blake and Andrea sole ownership. Blake says that the copurchase of the home was a way for his parents to "help us out and get started, so to speak." In the initial purchase of the townhouse and during their co-ownership, Blake's family gave them approximately $90,000 to $100,000 toward the house. Blake's family got a tax break as co-owners. Blake says he could not have purchased the townhouse without what he called an "interesting arrangement" with his father. "They actually threw money, as a stipend, to us. And then for money that they gave us, we gave them back tax shelter, tax advantages as co-owners."

Blake acknowledged that family financial help and his parents' cosigning of the mortgage were indispensable to getting them started. I asked Blake in 1998 the impolite question of how much money they had inherited already. "It's a horrendous number, it's scary. I'm guessing between ninety and a hundred thousand dollars."

By 2000 their young boys were growing, and like most growing families, they wanted more space, so they sold their townhouse, used the considerable equity that had built up for a sizeable down payment, and bought a four-bedroom townhouse right in the same neighborhood for $375,000.

Our 2010 conversation with Blake and Andrea revealed that the family's income had been stable, with Blake's $125,000 salary having slightly less purchasing power than his 1998 salary. Blake had taken a mandatory pay cut as the Great Recession hit the global pharmaceutical company he worked for. But the Millses were not treading water; their wealth was rising. In 1998, their net wealth was $118,000; by 2010, it had more than quintupled to $632,000, a wealth increase driven by their home equity. Excluding home equity, their net financial assets in 2010 were $330,000, up from $87,000 in 1998—a very respectable but less dramatic increase. Blake's employer-sponsored pension investments and IRAs helped to drive the rise in their financial wealth.

The family's children were doing well in the local public school district. The older, Andy, was about to start college at a state university, and the younger, Mark, was starting his sophomore year in high school. In 2001, as the young boys were just starting school, the Millses had decided that Andrea would quit working and become a stay-at-home mom. They wanted one parent closely involved in their sons' education. When we talked in 2010, Andrea had gone back to work part-time, since the boys were getting older and transitioning to college.

The Mills family's wealth seemed ample and included mutual funds Andrea's parents had set up for the two boys' college education in 1998. Yet Andrea was uneasy about the family's future economic security, largely due to the cost of college. She was stunned by the tuition at the public university where Andy was enrolling; she and Blake had both graduated from state universities in California when tuition was negligible, but the state university system had raised tuition by more than 450 percent over the previous fifteen years. This huge tuition hike reflects soaring college costs nationwide, which have far outstripped pay increases and often stress family finances and burden the next generation with debt. (The average student loan debt in California's state university system is now $18,460.) The funds her parents had established would pay for about one year of Andy's tuition. With college costs in mind, Andrea was looking for full-time work again, but had not found it when we talked.[15] Andrea's bind, pitting future economic security against financial support for children's higher education, has become emblematic of the squeeze on middle-class families. In the Millses' case, inheritance mitigates the dilemma because they can pursue both, though Andrea's sticker shock and concern are still real.

By 2015, the value of their home had risen to $868,000[16]—a return of nearly $500,000 leveraged from the initial $90,000 to $100,000 investment from Blake's family. The Mills family serves as a good example of the difficulty of distinguishing inheritance from subsequent wealth accumulation. Was their $500,000 of additional home equity the result of their savvy in real estate markets or contingent upon their inheritance? Others, no doubt, might have squandered this inheritance, as a couple of families we talked to indeed did. But the large majority of American families do not have $100,000 inheritances to invest in homes or other assets or to squander. And while the amount of the Mills family's inheritance is pretty typical for white families that do inherit, recall that the much smaller number of black families who inherit also receive considerably less. An inheritance of $100,000 would be extraordinarily rare for a black family; as noted earlier, one in ten are fortunate enough to inherit, and half receive less than $52,000. We must recognize not only how inheritance can change lives but also whose lives are more likely to be transformed by such legacies, because advantage and inequality are different sides of the same process.

The Mills children will attend a very respectable university, while the system will play out differently for less fortunate young adults. Among other tremendous advantages, inheritance helps pass along significantly higher chances of obtaining a college degree, which in turn leads to higher-paying careers and much higher lifetime earnings, lower unemployment rates and poverty levels, and better health and longer lives. Individuals from the highest-income families were eight times more likely than individuals from low-income families to obtain a bachelor's degree by age twenty-four, according to a recent study.[17] We have seen already that wealthier families have the ability to support their children's higher education and do so. This massive rich-poor divide in bachelor's degree attainment is now the largest it's been since the early 1970s. Wealth and inheritance pass the advantages of upper-middle-class status from parents to children. Those not born into such wealth and privilege are more often stuck in the status of their birth—the essence of toxic inequality.

Inheritance is not just a key driver of toxic inequality; it is also the enemy of equal opportunity and meritocracy. Nevertheless, government policies in the United States have long guaranteed the ability to easily pass the unearned advantages, surplus opportunities, and singular privileges that accompany family wealth to subsequent generations. Carline Clark told us how she was "constantly physically in touch with [her parents'] money, and able to manipulate it"—in part "so that it doesn't all go to Estate Tax." But in fact, the estate tax offers a prime example of how policy favors a few wealthy families at the expense of opportunity for the many. In 2016 a tax filing was required whenever estate wealth for a single individual exceeded $5,450,000. For a couple, $10,900,000 was excluded. Estate wealth over that amount was then taxed at 40 percent. Since the early 2000s, the exclusion levels have increased steadily, while the tax rates have declined; in 2001, only estates under $675,000 were excluded, and wealth over that amount was then subject to a 55 percent tax rate. The richest can now pass along a lot more while paying less. And in reality the tax affects only an infinitesimal number of estates. In 2011, when $5 million was excluded, only 18 out of every 10,000 adults who passed away had estates large enough to pay any estate tax. Yet many continue to argue for abolishing the estate tax entirely, suggesting that taxing wealth destroys initiative.

Inheritance could be characterized as the nemesis of equal opportunity, meritocracy, the American ideal, and quite possibly democracy itself. It poses a severe threat to our nation's foundational ideas of fair play, achievement, and playing by the rules. Yet many defend the privileges of the 2 out of every 1,000 families who leave untaxed millions upon millions of unearned wealth to their children. And as the next chapter will show, the ever-narrowing estate tax is just one way in which America's tax code and other government policies disproportionately help—not hurt—those who have wealth already.

THE HIDDEN HAND
OF GOVERNMENT

THE PRECEDING CHAPTERS HAVE EXPLAINED WHY WEALTH matters for families and then traced how some families build wealth in their homes and neighborhoods, through their jobs, and via inheritance. At each step of the way, the often hidden hand of government also exerts a powerful force. US government policies are a major driver of toxic inequality, privileging those who have wealth already, making its accumulation harder for those who lack it, and allowing living standards to fall for families who get by on paychecks alone. Federal tax expenditures and other provisions of the tax code disproportionately benefit wealthy home owners, workers with employer-sponsored retirement plans and generous employer-subsidized health coverage, heirs to large estates, and students at affluent private colleges—even as government investments that support typical American families are curtailed.

Direct government policies or programs like Temporary Assistance for Needy Families, unemployment insurance, and health care have been intensely debated in the public square, while tax code provisions and tax expenditures receive far less attention.

Thomas Piketty's landmark *Capital in the Twenty-First Century* argued that we have entered an era in which gains from wealth—whether in the form of stocks, bonds, or property—outpace economic growth. In this new era, the wealthy continue to grow even wealthier, partly because they have the means to shape policy to work ever more efficiently in their favor at the expense of everybody else. And indeed, scholars and journalists, including Robert Reich, Joseph Stiglitz, and David Cay Johnston, have begun to document the numerous ways in which very wealthy individuals, large corporations, and the financial industry have rewritten the rules of the US economy since the early 1970s, successfully shifting the balance of power between public and private interests in areas ranging from estate taxes to health care to housing finance reform to retirement security to social assistance.[1] Such changes have deepened inequality, and many have remained largely hidden from view and thus absent from public discourse.

Direct public spending and government programs form the visible tip of the policy "iceberg" and are the almost exclusive focus of public debate. The submerged bulk of public policy, meanwhile, includes special favors provided through the tax code and the rules and regulations that shape the US economy, determine growth, and affect the sharing of prosperity.[2] Together, the result is historic levels of wealth inequality alongside a cavernous and growing racial wealth gap. This chapter details some of the ways in which the policy landscape—from government programs to tax expenditures to new economic rules—shapes the lives of American families and drives America's toxic inequality.

Toxic inequality may seem unavoidable since the rules that help create it are largely obscured, iceberg-like, shielded by taken-for-granted assumptions, and formulated outside formal democratic channels. But because public policy choices largely drive toxic inequality, it is not actually inevitable or intransigent. Today's policies mark a significant departure from those of the past, and the very people and corporations who benefit from them the most have advocated for them effectively. We need only look closely to see how policy privileges the wealthy to the detriment of the country's overall well-being, actively subverting our democratic aspirations and increasing wealth and racial wealth divisions.

Let's start with Lindsay Bonde, a woman coping with sudden life-changing circumstances, whose savings were depleted at least in part by federal policy more intent on protecting corporate interests than helping families. When we interviewed her in 1998, Lindsay was working as a full-time adult education counselor in addition to performing a few jobs on the side to bring in extra money. She described growing up poor and white in a predominately black and Hispanic neighborhood in one of Boston's housing projects, where she experienced first-hand court-ordered school desegregation and the tumultuous busing solution. She became committed to bettering life for all children and ended up becoming a community activist, working with a local community development corporation to rebuild her diversified neighborhood. Lindsay counted herself among the "working poor" and wanted her three children to be "higher" than that. By 1998, she and her common-law husband were separated but still shared the house and family expenses. Her net financial wealth was $25,000.

When we talked again in 2010 her three children were all grown up, college educated, working good jobs, and out of the house. She was divorced, had a life insurance policy and stock market investments, and held $3,000 in a savings account. Lindsay's ascent from the working poor to middle-income status had peaked in 2007 with an income of $47,000 and net wealth close to $75,000, including her share of home equity. In impressive ways this poor, white woman had broken into the middle class and saw her children start their adult lives in far better circumstances than she had, just as she hoped.

But her life took a sudden turn for the worse. Her middle-class status collapsed in 2007, when, after working for twenty-two years as an educational counselor, she was diagnosed with osteoporosis, had to have spinal surgery, and could no longer work. Her disability meant she could no longer climb the stairs to her part of the house, which she still shared with her former husband. Using her share of home equity as a large down payment, Lindsay purchased a home in a modest Boston community that could better accommodate her limited mobility.

Unable to work and requiring powerful medicines for her chronic and debilitating condition, she saw her income cut nearly in half to $29,000, and because she had worked for over two decades and contributed to Social Security, most of her income came from Social Security Disability Insurance. Her insurance copayments, out-of-pocket medical expenses, and transportation to appointments cost her $200 a month.

A lot came undone for Lindsay Bonde. With her income nearly halved, amid rising medical costs, she started to accumulate large credit card debt ($9,000) and began withdrawing funds from savings and investment accounts. By 2010, excluding a life insurance policy and a retirement account, she owed $100 more in credit card debt than the combined money in her savings account and the value of the stocks she still owned. It appeared unlikely that her depleting wealth could continue to protect her against emergencies or unexpected expenses. Moving forward, Lindsay is most concerned about her health and associated medical costs; she hopes to remain independent and not to become a drain on her children's resources.

One key factor in Lindsay Bonde's slide from the middle class was the terms set by government policy on which she could receive the drugs essential to treat her degenerative osteoporosis. Americans now pay higher prices for medicine than people in any other advanced nation. On average Humira, often prescribed for her condition, costs over $1,900 per month in the United States compared to less than $1,000 in New Zealand; it is more expensive in America than in any advanced country. Drugs like this are so much more expensive in the United States due to the effective influence of the pharmaceutical industry on policy and rules. Medicare Part D, for example, implemented in 2006 to provide better coverage for seniors and people with disabilities like Lindsay Bonde, covers nearly 40 million people. Despite being the largest federal drug program, in rules written at the behest of the pharmaceutical industry, Medicare is not allowed to "interfere with the negotiations" between drug companies and plan sponsors or pharmacies. Thus the federal program is prohibited from using its purchasing power to buy needed drugs at better prices because it orders huge quantities.[3] This key provision prohibits government from negotiating the lowest possible price—which is what the Veterans Administration (VA) does. It's what every business owner does. It's what every other industrialized nation does for the universal health care of its citizens.[4] Corporate and financial elite power trumps the obvious, practical, and healthy choice.

As a result brand-name drugs cost Medicare Part D twice the median price of the same drugs in the thirty-one democratic and market-oriented countries of the Organization for Economic Cooperation and Development. Medicare pays 73 and 80 percent more, respectively, than Medicaid and the VA, which have more leeway in leveraging lower drug costs for larger purchases. This leads Medicare to pay approximately $16 billion more a year than if it could negotiate the same prices as Medicaid and the VA.[5] Instead of saving money for the public and the people who require these drugs, rewritten rules deliver $16 billion more in profits to drug companies.

The legislation and other rules protecting pharmaceutical companies' profits at the public expense were crafted out of public view and manipulated so that virtually no accountability or public scrutiny could take place.[6] Lindsay Bonde's health and medical needs and those of millions like her were not represented; nor was the public interest. As her life circumstances changed and as policy failed to support or protect her, the high cost of essential medications quickly exhausted Lindsay's life savings, built from twenty-two years of hard work. Government policies contributed crucially to

Lindsay's financial descent, growing vulnerability, and declining ability to take care of herself.

WE SPOKE TO ANOTHER WOMAN WHOSE EXPERIENCE ILLUS-trates the effect of federal tax policy on average families. When we first talked to Reese Otis in 1998, she was finishing her PhD in Boston and married to a legal aid attorney. The two divorced, and a few years later she reconnected with a childhood friend who was living in Los Angeles and working at a consulting firm. Both hailed from South Carolina, and when they married, they decided to move back there to raise their two daughters from previous marriages. In 2003, they bought and remodeled a house together on an island a short ferry ride from the mainland. Reese—who was forty-six when we spoke with her in 2010—grew up on the island and was thrilled to be back.

Armed with a PhD, Reese had taken a job in 1998 working for a foundation focused on housing, refugee settlements, and immigration throughout the world. She slowly worked her way up, taking various positions over the course of twelve years, and continued to work remotely for the foundation after moving back to the Southeast. Just before we spoke in 2010, she had voluntarily accepted a generous severance package from the foundation and changed careers, starting by teaching a few courses part-time.

Reese had achieved considerable economic and professional mobility in her lifetime, even while her family income had fluctuated widely as both she and her husband moved among full-time work, part-time jobs, and periods without paid employment. When we spoke in 2010, Reese and her husband—who are both white—enjoyed two incomes and counted on occasional help from their families. Their combined income was $80,000—above the median but squarely in the middle class. Reese expressed some anxiety, however, about having hardly any savings for retirement; indeed, she and her husband had few assets besides their house and no investments.

The Otises' income came exclusively from their paychecks. As a result, they typify how federal tax policies favor wealth over earnings and thereby actively disadvantage over 45 million middle-income families like this one. After accounting for some standard deductions, Reese and her husband would pay a composite tax rate of 14 percent on their $80,000 income, yielding a federal income tax of about $11,500. The dollars and cents would look very different for a family that had the same amount of annual income from proceeds on invested capital rather than paid work. Assuming a healthy return, such a family would need to have invested approximately $1.6 million to net $80,000 in income—and because of the difference in the capital gains and income tax rates, they would pay just $765 in taxes to the Internal Revenue Service (IRS), a difference of over $10,000.

The disparity is even greater for higher-income families. About one in twenty families bring in $200,000 or more a year from their jobs, an income that places them in the top 5 percent of earners. In 2015, a couple with a combined income of $200,000, with no investments or other income, would pay a composite 22 percent tax rate, assuming they did not use deductions to reduce their liability or other tricks to hide their wages. Their income would yield $43,000 or so in tax revenues for the federal government. A family who did nothing other than invest its wealth in stocks or property, receiving $200,000 in returns, would owe significantly less. Their $200,000 gain would be taxed at the lower capital gains rate, with the first $75,000 tax free, a 15 percent tax rate on earnings up to $464,000, and a 20 percent rate on earnings above that figure. The second family would be taxed at a blended rate of 9 percent, yielding the government about $18,000 in tax revenues. The difference between paychecks and profits from wealth is stark: $43,000 in taxes compared to $18,000, a tax rate of 22 percent versus 9 percent. What's more, amassing $200,000 from wealth alone would require that the family have at least $4 million in financial wealth to begin with. The far wealthier family would pay less than half the taxes paid by the high-earning, less wealthy family.

The point is not to suggest that the amount of taxes paid is too low or too high in these particular examples. A family with $200,000 in income is likely to have investments, just as a family earning $200,000 from investments is likely to have income from work. Rather, these examples demonstrate how public policy in the United States favors income from wealth over pay from work and how prioritizing wealth over paychecks in this way exacerbates wealth inequality and contributes to toxic inequality. Even with some public discussion about who pays what effective tax rate during presidential election campaigns, the policy process takes place mostly out of sight because there is barely any public discussion or understanding of wealth, much less of arcane-sounding tax rules. Public and political attention is still riveted on income.

The tax code is just one of many government measures that protect and expand wealth for the already wealthy, even as it and other government policies penalize those trying to scrape together an emergency nest egg.

IN CURRENT THINKING ABOUT GOVERNMENT POLICY AND ITS effect on the distribution of economic resources, the flow of income to individuals and families gets far more attention than their wealth. Most families do not have enough wealth to merit concern with policies affecting it. Yet government plays an enormously important role in providing wealth escalators to some, shaping how wealth is accumulated and distributed among groups, and determining how it is valued. The US tax code, in addition to taxing income from work and from wealth at hugely different rates, thereby advantaging wealth already amassed, also subsidizes wealth accumulation for wealthy individuals and families in other ways. (This discussion leaves aside the ways laws are written to favor corporations, but a constellation of public subsidies allows highly profitable corporations to reduce their tax liabilities, costing taxpayers in excess of $155 billion every year.[7])

These features of today's tax code are just the latest manifestation of America's long history of policies that use public resources to enable private wealth generation through property acquisition, home ownership, business development, and higher education. This phenomenon is distinct from the sort of social assistance at the core of the modern welfare state, which provides a safety net designed to ensure that families do not starve, find themselves homeless, or have to do without emergency medical care or heat in the winter. Today, to receive such support, families typically must prove they meet certain criteria and then behave in the prescribed manner. Rules often penalize families with loss of eligibility if they begin to save money for a child's education or for their own retirement. For instance, eligibility for food stamps is contingent on not having a savings account with more than a few thousand dollars. Such impossible choices make escaping poverty more difficult and *discourage* wealth generation. We impose these choices on poor families and no one else, and we should not do so.

To truly see how the US government fosters the generation of private wealth, one must look not at social assistance programs for those in need but instead at what I call the wealth budget of the government as a whole—the full range of policies and tax code provisions that enable wealth generation through public investments. Historically, notable examples of such investments include land granted to colonists, the Mexican Cession of 1848, the Homestead Act of 1862, and the Land-Grant College Acts of 1862 and 1890. Each of these actions provided public lands for purposes that were considered public goods: ownership of property, the creation of new businesses, and the formation of institutions of higher education. But these worthy public-good investments also enabled individuals to build private wealth. The Homestead Act of 1862, for example, offered land free to those who could build a shelter on and earn a livelihood off of the land. It covered approximately 20 percent of all public lands at the time, and some 45 million Americans today are descendants of homesteaders, but it benefitted remarkably few African

Americans or other minorities.[8] The Land-Grant College Acts of 1862 and 1890 gave public land to establish colleges that would teach agricultural and industrial skills, many of which became the flagship institutions of state university systems. Over seventy institutions of higher education today got their start in this way. But even though they were designated for the public good, discriminatory laws and customs systematically excluded African Americans from most of these colleges and universities (with the exception of a few set aside for African Americans only) for nearly one hundred years.

In the twentieth century, robust wealth-enabling policies continued to build wealth platforms for economic mobility and security for some. For instance, the National Housing Act of 1934 was passed to make housing and mortgages more affordable. The institutions it established, such as the Federal Housing Administration (FHA) and the Federal Savings and Loan Insurance Corporation, form the backbone of the modern mortgage and home-building industries. The law changed how white families could buy homes, replacing large out-of-pocket down payments and high-interest, short-term loans with low down payments and long-term, thirty-year mortgages at reasonable interest rates. Providing mortgage insurance and financial services also helped to establish new market rules for lending and home buying. These new rules and institutions put home ownership within the reach of America's burgeoning middle class in the prosperous years after World War II. The home ownership rate rose from 43.6 percent in 1940 to 69 percent right before the Great Recession and housing implosion.[9] Housing equity accounts for approximately two-thirds of net wealth among middle-income families, and in very real ways, the economic security of America's middle class rests on the wealth built up in home equity. The National Housing Act of 1934 made it all possible.

At the same time, implementation of the National Housing Act legitimized and hardened the residential segregation, inner-city-concentrated poverty, and spatial isolation that characterized America's housing patterns. In a process known as redlining, FHA administrators created a system of maps that rated neighborhoods according to stability criteria based on race, ethnicity, and income. Integrated neighborhoods were classified as unstable, and neighborhoods with black populations were colored red and virtually excluded from FHA-insured mortgages. This form of institutionalized racism dominated the housing market from 1934 until 1968, and much of it lives on today, although more informally and implicitly. This policy is, arguably, not only the source of much white American middle-class wealth but also a fundamental contemporary pillar of the racial wealth gap in the United States.[10]

Since our inception as a nation, our priorities have been clear. We have provided some groups opportunities to homestead, own property and homes, get an education, and earn a livelihood, but for centuries these policies, by intent and implementation, virtually excluded Native Americans and minority groups. The government's wealth budget has a long history of serving as a core wealth-building system for some while denying others the same chances. And yet millions upon millions of Americans benefited, and continue to benefit, from land-grant colleges and the Homestead Act, despite their limitations. As clearly racist as their exclusions may have been, these policies were nevertheless both visionary and effective for large swaths of the white population. That level of robust big thinking and inclusiveness is altogether missing today. In contrast, the government's wealth budget even more narrowly benefits those least in need and excludes the many.

The government's role in reforming the home-buying market postrecession is further shaping the rules of ownership and wealth accumulation. Recall India Medina and her family, who owned a home in a St. Louis neighborhood where houses have lost half their value since 2007. Let's see how families like the Medinas purchased homes in the past, how those rules are being rewritten, and the influence of major financial institutions in advocating changes for their own benefit. Most families like the Medinas purchased homes backed by Fannie Mae or Freddie Mac, government-sponsored enterprises established to stimulate the housing market by backing more affordable mortgages for moderate- to low-income families. When the Medinas bought their home in 1999, Fannie and Freddie secured slightly over 40 percent of mortgages; following the 2007 collapse of the housing market and tightening of credit, Fannie and Freddie now back 80 percent of the nation's mortgages and an even larger share of homes among low- and moderate-income families. CitiFinancial originated the Medinas' mortgage, which it then sold to Fannie Mae. Without this secondary mortgage market, banks, thrifts, and credit unions would be holding long-term debt and unable to underwrite or fund new home purchases, education loans, business start-ups and expansions, and so forth. The home loan market weighed in at $5.7 trillion in 2015, with $9.4 trillion in outstanding mortgage debt owed by families.[11] Mortgages purchased by Fannie and Freddie must meet strict criteria, meant at least in theory to minimize the number of risky loans offered to families. Freddie Mac helped 14.7 million families purchase or rent homes between 2009 and September 2015.[12] Among the mortgages backed by Fannie and Freddie, more than 2.7 million loan workouts have been completed since 2009. Indeed there is compelling evidence that Freddie and Fannie standards result in more affordable and stable home ownership. At least six families we interviewed had successfully modified their loans, negotiating new and affordable terms to keep the foreclosure wolf from their door and the family in the home. The delinquency rate for single families whose payments are more than sixty days past due is 15.1 percent for those with subprime mortgages compared to 1.5 percent for Freddie Mac loan holders.

In September 2008, Fannie Mae and Freddie Mac were placed into conservatorship as the nation's housing market was severely damaged in the foreclosure crisis, leaving them and many too-big-to-fail banks on the brink of collapse. The Treasury gave Fannie and Freddie $187.5 billion to stabilize them; they had repaid that bailout in full plus contributed another $53.8 billion in profits by the end of 2015. With the dominant players still in conservatorship and waiting for new rules, the housing finance market has been broken ever since, severely impacting all but particularly low- and moderate-income families and families of color.

Financial elites, the Bankers Mortgage Association, big banks, and lobbyists are aggressively stepping in to determine what the housing finance market will look like moving forward. A thorough investigative report in the *New York Times* in late 2015 documented a concerted Wall Street effort to take over the mortgage market and "privatize the nation's broken home mortgage system."[13] The *Times* account is based on a review of lobbying records, legal filings, internal e-mails and memos, housing officials' calendars, and White House and Treasury visitor logs. The proposed housing finance reform would reduce and wind down Freddie and Fannie's role in the mortgage market. The effort to "eliminate Fannie and Freddie was a page out of the mortgage bankers' playbook towards a more 'bank-centric model' benefiting larger institutions." In 2016 the housing mortgage market had not been fixed yet, but financial elites are mightily engaged in reforming it for their own huge financial benefit. They already have influenced the viable options under consideration to swing the market balance toward themselves. If this campaign to eviscerate Fannie and Freddie and radically shift the balance to big banks succeeds, then purchasing a home will become far more difficult for families like the Medinas.

As it does with home ownership, American society materially encourages other public goods—such as retirement savings, higher education, and entrepreneurship—primarily through tax expenditures: reductions in tax liability for a particular class of taxpayers intended to promote policy goals that benefit society. The government has in its toolbox the ability to use revenues and spending to promote valued economic behaviors (e.g., saving, investing in a business) for the greater good of all. It values behaviors in a market economy because individual achievements in these areas are said to add to overall societal stability, security, competitiveness, innovation, and well-being. Some contend, for example, that a home owner is more engaged in her community than a renter.[14]

Like social assistance and other direct spending programs, tax expenditures function as entitlements for those who meet the established criteria.[15] There is a difference, however. If a Department of Housing and Urban Development (HUD) program encouraged home ownership by sending home owners checks that matched a portion of their mortgage interest payments, this would be considered a spending program and would face scrutiny and debate every year as part of the federal budget process. In fact, however, as the IRS administers the mortgage interest deduction, it subsidizes home ownership through targeted tax benefits. Because it gets accounted for in the federal budget as a tax reduction, not a spending program, the subsidy is not subjected to annual scrutiny and the accompanying political bloviating. It and similar expenditures are far more removed from the democratic process than spending programs and are thus harder to reform.

All told, tax expenditures in the 2014 fiscal year reduced federal revenue from income and payroll taxes by over $1.2 trillion.[16] The government distributes more public resources invisibly through tax expenditures than it spends on much more visible programs like Social Security, or on the combined cost of Medicare and Medicaid, or on defense. Through this largely below-the-surface mechanism, public resources are used to solidify and expand the already deeply entrenched advantages of wealth.

Consider housing. If asked to describe American housing policy, the average person would almost surely answer that the government spends massive amounts of money on public and subsidized housing for poor and low-income families. Yet this is not the case. Federal housing programs began in the 1930s with public housing developments owned and operated by the government. Over time, these original efforts have been joined by a large number of other programs that subsidize privately built and operated housing developments and provide housing vouchers for tenants to live in private units of their own choosing. In all, we devote about $40 billion a year to means-tested housing programs for low-income and homeless families.[17] By contrast, in 2015, the public invested $205.6 billion in home ownership. Over the six years from 2012 to 2017, $1.2 trillion will have been dedicated to subsidize home ownership, mostly through the mortgage interest tax deduction that permits home owners to deduct from their tax liability the interest paid on their mortgages.[18] We invest five times more public money in home ownership for families that can afford homes than in decent, affordable housing for those who cannot.

Furthermore, this public investment in home ownership flows mostly to the best-off home owners, redistributing wealth at the top, driving wealth inequality, and contributing to toxic inequality. One set of estimates calculated that the top 10 percent of taxpayers reaped 86 percent of the total distributed through the mortgage interest deduction.[19] The Tax Policy Center's model calculated that the top 20 percent of taxpayers reaped 72 percent of the annual subsidy. Either way, the inescapable fact is that the best-off benefit at the expense of the majority. Indeed, a family in the top 1 percent of income earners receives an average $6,116 subsidy from the mortgage interest deduction, while a middle-income home owner like Reese Otis receives a modest $183 on average. Adding in federal tax deductions claimed for state and local property taxes swells the average public subsidy among the top 1 percent to over $10,000.

Meanwhile, many home owners are excluded from the subsidy entirely. The Medinas were one such family, and they owed more on the home than they could sell it for. As they approached retirement, their home was the largest single asset they controlled, critical both for shelter and for their economic security. Arguably, they were ideal candidates for the public good of housing stability. But collecting $62,000 per year from paychecks, they were not poor enough to qualify for housing assistance. And not a dollar of the over $200 billion in home ownership subsidies delivered each year through the tax code reaches them either. Taking the mortgage interest deduction would require the Medinas to itemize deductions, and their mortgage interest payments and other deductions were not greater than the $12,600 standard deduction for a family. Only 35 percent of those in their tax bracket itemize deductions. If HUD paid out the mortgage interest deduction, then the Medinas might qualify for both it and the standard deduction. Home ownership subsidies delivered through the tax code are simply not designed for moderate-income families like theirs.[20]

Unlike the Medinas, two of every three filers with $75,000 or more in income itemized their tax returns in 2014.[21] This is one of several reasons that housing subsidies flow to high-income, least-in-need home owners. Not only are high-income families far more likely to itemize deductions on their taxes, but home ownership deductions are also pegged to the family's tax bracket, with deductions being worth more in the higher tax brackets. With the same mortgage amounts, this means that someone with $150,000 in income in the 28 percent tax bracket could get a bigger deduction than someone with $80,000 in income in the 25 percent tax bracket. Taxpayers can deduct the interest paid on first and second mortgages up to $1 million in mortgage debt (the limit is $500,000 if married and filing separately). Any interest paid on first or second mortgages over this amount is not tax deductible. Furthermore, high-income families buy more expensive homes, taking out bigger mortgages and thus paying more interest eligible for tax deduction. In addition, the first $500,000 (for a couple) gained from selling a primary residence is exempted from taxation, and gains over that amount are subject to the 14 percent capital gains tax rate. And families in high-income tax brackets, say 33 percent ($230,000 to $412,000 for a couple), benefit most from capital gains exclusions because the tax liability from profit in excess of $500,000 from home sales is thus 19 percent lower than the tax liability if it were income.

The mortgage interest deduction is just one mechanism through which public investment flows to the wealthy at tax time. Another relates to the tax code's treatment of retirement savings. Earlier, we met the Ackerman family, whose largest reservoir of wealth is an employer-sponsored retirement savings plan with matching benefits. When we interviewed her, we learned that Allison Ackerman contributed $3,000 annually to the retirement account, and her employer added another $5,100. All of this money—treated as pretax and not reported as income until she retires and begins drawing from the account—was shielded from tax liability. Assuming the family was in the 25 percent tax bracket, this retirement package amounted to a $2,025 tax subsidy. If Allison had not had access to her employer-sponsored account and invested the same $3,000, the Ackermans' actual income taxes would increase by about $750 and thus reduce her after-tax paycheck. The tax-shielded status of these contributions should be seen as a public investment producing private wealth, no different from the expenditures that flow toward home owners. It has enabled the Ackermans to feel comfortable and helped them over their working years to build a retirement nest egg of $350,000.

This public investment is not nearly as undemocratic as the incentives benefitting wealthy home owners. Inclusive, employer-sponsored, mandatory, and matched savings vehicles for retirement indeed ought to be encouraged by government policy and supported with public resources, for they can help move typical American families forward and bolster economic security. The problem, again, is that right now the supporting mechanism of saving for retirement with pretax money, a problem magnified if matching money is involved, mostly benefits those working at large organizations, and, as we have seen, minorities, women, immigrants, and low-paid workers are less likely to find jobs with such employers. All told, federal tax subsidies for retirement benefits will rise to $180 billion in 2016. And as with the mortgage interest deduction, over two-thirds (68 percent) of that amount accrues to the top one-fifth of earners. The top 10 percent get over half (51 percent) of the tax subsidies for employer-based retirement account payments. This translates to an average $12,000 entitlement for the top 1 percent of earners and $363 for a family in the middle.[22] As a result, the distribution of public benefits still tilts in a distorted fashion to the top and most often to whites.

A similar mechanism and off-kilter distribution applies to health insurance. When workers participate in an employer-sponsored health insurance plan, their pretax contribution to the cost of coverage is not tax liable. This public investment, intended to encourage broader health-care coverage, cost taxpayers $155 billion in 2016, not including revenue lost to Social Security.[23] When an employer pays for part or all of a worker's coverage, that benefit is not counted as income, and there is no cap on how large it can be. The Patient Protection and Affordable Care Act (commonly called the Affordable Care Act or, colloquially, Obamacare) included a provision that will recover public revenues on very high-cost plans starting in 2018. Workers whose employers provide health insurance—typically those who work at large companies or organizations, like the Ackermans—receive the added benefit of paying for health insurance with pretax money. Roughly 160 million Americans get their health insurance through their employers. In 2014, 8 million tax filers claimed medical deductions, and filers with incomes over $100,000 received 62 percent of the total benefit, making the distributional impact somewhat less tilted to the very wealthy.[24]

The data are abundantly clear that tax expenditures actively redistribute wealth to the top while skipping those

low- and moderate-income families most in need of building up assets. However, because race and ethnicity data are
not collected on tax forms, we have less direct information
about the racial distribution of tax expenditures or their impact on the racial wealth gap. But research clearly suggests
this impact is substantial. In one study, the Tax Policy Center
examined zip codes in which high rates of residents claimed
the mortgage interest deduction. It found that African Americans represent only 5.6 percent of the population in these
areas, less than half their national proportion.[25] Residents of
zip codes with the highest rates of taxpayers claiming the
deduction—where big federal dollars flow to subsidize home
ownership—are disproportionately white, middle-aged, and
married. Another way of getting a handle on the nexus of
race and tax expenditures is to analyze expenditures by income brackets, since we know the exact percentage of African
Americans in each income bracket. This blunt method shows
that African Americans receive only 3.5 percent of public investments via tax expenditures in individual wealth building,
when they comprise 13.2 percent of the population. Using
the 2014 estimate[26] that wealth-building tax expenditures
total nearly $400 billion annually, this means that the tax
code delivers a whopping $35 billion discriminatory race pen-
alty each year. African American families would accumulate
$35 billion more in wealth each year if their incomes were
distributed according to their national representation—13.2
percent in each income bracket. Projecting that one-year figure out to the Tax Policy Center's six-year estimate of $2.5
trillion in public investment in home ownership, retirement
security, small business development, and other areas via tax

expenditures suggests a massive structural race deficit.[27] The African American share of this investment falls over $200 billion short of African Americans' demographic representation. This is a clear case of policy shutting the door to wealth for African Americans and other people of color.

THE PRIVILEGING OF GAINS FROM WEALTH OVER INCOME FROM work at tax time and the huge public investment via tax expenditures in wealth-building for the affluent are two of the largest policy mechanisms directing wealth to the top. But the best-known and most contentious public policy related to wealth in the United States is no doubt the estate tax. Accurate understanding of this tax is the exception rather than the rule, however. Nearly half of Americans surveyed, 49 percent, believed that most families have to pay the tax, and another one in five said they did not know enough to hazard a guess.[28] This is nowhere near accurate, and one report has suggested that accurate information about the tax, framed with equity arguments, lifts popular support for the tax from 40 to 62 percent.[29]

Its opponents, who suggest that the estate tax imperils vulnerable family farms, small businesses, and community newspapers when their owners die, actively cultivate this misunderstanding. With a theatrical flourish, Republican congressional leaders once delivered legislation to abolish federal estate taxes on a red tractor driven by a farmer.[30] Opponents also enlist African American small newspaper owners to testify that they will lose the family business unless the estate tax is abolished or radically altered. But the facts are quite different: a renowned investigative reporter could not find a single documented case of a family forced to sell its farm to pay estate taxes, and no African American community newspaper has been sold for this reason either.[31] In fact, only 18 in every 10,000 deaths involve estates large enough to fall within the current estate tax provisions,[32] and a small band of America's richest families leads the charge to repeal it. Nine families owning approximately $137 billion in assets have lobbied directly on the estate tax in the last few years; one estimate holds that they would save between $25 billion and $55 billion, depending on how significantly the tax rate was reduced.[33] Some of America's wealthiest families actively cultivate misunderstanding of the estate tax and push for outright repeal. These families own some of America's best-known brand names and businesses, from candy companies to greeting cards to car rentals to supermarkets to oil to beauty products. Several superrich families invested $10.4 million in lobbying and public campaigns between 2012 and 2015. Bolstering these wealthy families' sustained efforts, the Koch brothers began funding the crusade to kill the estate tax in 2015.[34]

Although the estate tax has survived thus far, its scope and progressivity have been dramatically reduced, with exclusion levels rising from $175,000 in the early 1980s to over $5.3 million in 2015 and with the top tax rate falling precipitously from 70 percent in the early 1980s to 40 percent in 2015.[35] As a result, only a tiny number of estates actually pay estate taxes. In 2013, less than 0.0002 percent of adults who passed away had estates large enough to pay any tax on them,[36] and the effective tax rate actually paid was under 15 percent. The current estate tax touches only one in five among the wealthiest 1 percent.

We met Carline Clark's family in Chapter 4. Her inherited family money did not approach that of the families that actively lobby on the estate tax, all of which are among the wealthiest ninety families in America, and we do not know if she contributed to this class effort. Perhaps she directed her energies elsewhere, as we saw her strategizing ways to legally avoid paying any gift or estate taxes. She kept close tabs on the law and knew that in 2015 an estate must be bigger than $10,000,000 before a filing was necessary. In 2001, around the time we first talked to Carline, only $675,000 was excluded, and estates then were subject to a 55 percent tax rate. The wealthy and their lobbyists and advocates have pushed up the tax-free exclusion dramatically while decreasing the tax rate. The richest now can pass along more at less cost. As an accountant who manages her parents' wealth and estate planning, Carline reports how she is "constantly physically in touch with their money, and able to manipulate it." She makes sure that some of the younger family members receive the tax-free maximum gift of $14,000 each year from her parents.

Operating alongside the narrowing estate tax are rules that exclude capital gains taxes on wealth investment at death— what tax attorneys and wonks call the "step-up basis." Under these rules, someone who inherits an investment that has appreciated in value since the day it was first purchased pays taxes only on proceeds that accrue from the day that person receives the asset and only if he or she sells it. Although some suggest the estate tax is double taxation—claiming that proceeds from investments like stocks have already been taxed—this is not necessarily the case.[37] Say your saintly and visionary grandmother invested $1,000 in Microsoft in 1986. After multiple stock splits, this investment would have netted around $575,000 in 2015. Had your grandmother died that year and sold the stock the year before her death, $574,000 in gains would be liable for capital gains tax. But if she did not sell and instead bequeathed the stock to you when she passed away, and if you sold it immediately, you would pay no capital gains tax because it had not appreciated over its value when you took ownership. In effect, holding stock until death exempts profits from capital gains tax, providing a huge and largely hidden tax benefit for the superrich. Like all tax expenditures, this represents revenue not available to the US Treasury, which must be raised instead through other taxes or cuts in services for the poor.

HIGHER EDUCATION IS CENTRAL TO THE AMERICAN DREAM OF social mobility, and evidence clearly shows that it can produce big changes. We have seen how it motivated the Otis, Arrora, Ackerman, and Mills families, although the challenges they faced and solutions they acted upon differed. Without a college degree, a child born into the lowest income quintile remains stuck there nearly three times more often than those who earn college degrees (45 versus 16 percent). The chances of long-distance mobility from the bottom to the top income quintile increase nearly fourfold for those with college degrees (19 versus 5 percent).[38] Particularly after World War II, policymakers charged higher education with aspirational, equity, and strategic goals to open opportunity more broadly and to position the United States for global leadership. President Harry S. Truman declared, "If the ladder of educational opportunity rises high at the doors of some youth and scarcely rises at the doors of others, while at the same time formal education is made a prerequisite to occupational and social advance, then education may become the means, not of eliminating race and class distinctions, but of deepening and solidifying them."[39] The promise of education has not worked out wholly as planned, as real educational outcomes that solidify inequality and the race and class divisions Truman warned about seem to have outmatched his lofty mobility aspirations and democratic ideals.

The proportion of higher education costs covered by state and local governments has declined sharply since before the Great Recession, continuing the trend of shifting responsibility for paying for college to students and parents. Nationwide, states spent 28 percent less on higher education in 2013 than in 2008, cuts directly correlated with cost increases borne by students and their parents and subsequent reductions in educational quality.[40] State and local governments accounted for 57 percent of higher education revenues in 1977, but covered just 39 percent in 2012. As a result, students and parents contributed about a third of the cost of education in 1977, but just under a half in 2012. Meanwhile, the share of higher education revenues provided by the federal government was $1 in every $8 in 2012, unchanged since 1980. The shift in funding from state and local governments to students and parents has occurred at a time when costs have risen dramatically and during a period when average wages have been static or declined in constant dollars. Taken together, these factors increase the short-term opportunity costs of higher education, especially for low- to middle-income students, compared to earnings they might generate by working.

Lower-income students and students of color are overrepresented in for-profit and public two-year institutions, while higher-income students are overrepresented in more prestigious universities with law and medical schools, advanced degree programs, and PhD programs.[41] Students from families in the highest income quartile are far more likely to attend private doctorate-granting institutions (26 percent), public doctorate-granting institutions (25 percent), and public four-year non-doctorate-granting institutions (26 percent). By comparison, students from the lowest income quartile represent more than half (57 percent) of students attending private for-profit four- and two-year institutions. A degree in business management from the for-profit Brown College in Minnesota will be less impressive to prospective employers and business associates than a business, entrepreneurship, and organizations degree from Brown University in Rhode Island, even if students graduate with the same skills.

The Federal Pell Grant program, which provides need-based grants to low-income undergraduate students, is the major policy tool for promoting access to postsecondary education. In 2011, 17.5 million students were enrolled in institutions of higher education, with over half (54 percent) receiving Pell Grants to help defray college costs. Three-fourths of all Pell Grant recipients for the 2010–2011 academic year had family incomes of $30,000 or less. But relative to the average cost of attendance, the value of the Pell Grant peaked in 1975, when the maximum grant covered 67 percent of average costs. But average tuition and fees at US colleges and universities have risen, in constant dollars, from $9,625 in 1970 to $20,234 in 2012–2013, more than doubling, and the maximum Pell Grant in 2012 was about 95 percent of the maximum in 1975. As a result, in 2012, the maximum Pell Grant covered only 27 percent of costs, the lowest percentage since the program's inception. This is part of the calculation that leads lower-income students to attend schools with lower average costs and reinforces educational tracking by wealth and income. Differences in tuition and costs for students in the highest and lowest family income quartiles have also increased since 1970, reflecting the increasingly stratified higher education system. It is reasonable to think that this propagates differences in education quality and greater market rewards for higher-priced educations, in which case the increasing gaps between college costs for students in the upper and lower family income quartiles reflect and exacerbate growing inequity.

The data on college attendance, graduation, and student debt paint a stark picture: 62 percent of whites, 52 percent of blacks, and 32 percent of Latinos start college at some point in their lives. Of those who enrolled in 2006, 30 percent of whites, 42 percent of Latinos, and 48 percent of blacks were unable to graduate from their programs within six years. But even though black and Latino families are underrepresented among the ranks of those who enroll in and complete college, they are overrepresented among the ranks of student debtors. Among young black households, with members aged twenty-five to forty, over half (54 percent) have student debt, compared to 39 percent of all young white households. Possibly due in part to lower overall rates of college attendance and graduation, one in five (20.7 percent) Latino families has student debt.[42] This millstone is a huge drag on asset accumulation, particularly for young adults. The big picture, including tuition, student grants, and loans, clearly evidences the public disinvestment at state and local levels, a leveling of federal investments, declining ability of Pell Grants to keep pace, and a cost shift to families and individuals. Burgeoning and debilitating debt and diverging college completion by income, wealth, and race have been the result.

Tax expenditures for higher education do even more to favor wealth and bake in inequality. The taxpaying public is bankrolling the education of students in the better-endowed and more selective schools to a far greater extent than they are supporting the education of students at state or regional universities or community colleges. Massive indirect subsidies through the tax code highly benefit elite educational institutions, whereas direct federal and state appropriations support state systems and community colleges. One commentator has scathingly characterized elite universities like Harvard and Princeton as hedge funds with an educational institution attached. Indeed, that indictment rings true when the money managers who administer huge university endowments get paid more than those endowments return to student financial aid. But if these private universities resemble hedge funds in some ways, they are publicly subsidized ones, because private educational institutions generally do not pay property tax, their endowment is free from taxation, donors are able to deduct their gifts from their own taxes, and financial gains from institutional investments are not taxed. In the previous chapter we discussed Andrea Mills's sticker shock at the cost of higher education. Andy Mills would be attending California State University, Fullerton, where the value of public investment per student (in both direct government support and tax subsidies) was $4,000. Meanwhile, students from wealthy families who attended Stanford four hundred miles north received much more in public subsidies: $63,000, or nearly sixteen times more, per student. Stanford's endowment, its annual gift receipts, and the value of the property it owns are all considerably larger than any of the California state universities' assets. The result is mammoth tax subsidies, further advantaging those who need them the least at the expense of those for whom public investment might make a difference in whether they complete college at all.[43]

Private universities are in fact so highly subsidized with public monies that it is inappropriate to think of them as private at all. Many of the richest universities in the country— sitting on hundreds of millions, often billions, in tax-exempt endowments and garnering tens of millions in tax-deductible gifts every year—receive government subsidies through current tax laws that dwarf anything received by the public colleges, universities, and community colleges that educate the majority of the nation's low- and middle-income students. For example, in 2013, Princeton University's tax-exempt status generated more than $100,000 per student in taxpayer subsidies, compared to around $12,000 (in both direct government appropriations and tax subsidies) at New Jersey's state flagship, Rutgers University, $4,700 per student at the nearby regional Montclair State University, and only $2,400 per student at Essex Community College.[44] Based on the tax exemptions and other government appropriations received, one report calculates that across the ten most highly endowed private institutions, taxpayers in 2013 spent more than $41,000 per student, nearly three times the average direct taxpayer support for students attending public flagship campuses in the same states as the private institutions. The wealthiest endowed colleges and universities, which need government subsidies the least, get the greatest subsidy per student. The affluent schools that receive higher subsidies educate a far lower percentage of low- and middle-income students than public institutions or private not-for-profit institutions with smaller endowments that receive far less support. Although the tax-exempt status of private not-for-profit institutions is meant to be a public benefit, the majority of taxpayers are poorly served by the tax-exempt status of large endowments at private colleges. Instead, government is bankrolling further inequality.[45]

TODAY, FEDERAL POLICY PRIVILEGES ALREADY-AMASSED WEALTH, redistributes opportunities to accumulate wealth to those at the top, and helps the wealthy maintain wealth over time and pass it along to their children. Meanwhile, it actively disadvantages those without any or much wealth and those who earn a living from paychecks alone. These policies have helped spawn the era of toxic inequality, producing a mounting racial wealth gap and historically high levels of wealth and income inequality. The culprits are not hard to find: wealthy elites, financial institutions, large corporations, and political leaders. Yet policy is man-made. If it is responsible for creating, amplifying, and maintaining toxic inequality, it is possible for us to reverse course. The next and final chapter articulates an agenda to do just that.

=6=

FORWARD TO EQUITY

I DIDN'T KNOW FULLY WHAT I WAS GETTING INTO WHEN I started this project two decades ago. I wanted to learn about how wealth shapes vital family choices and how assets affect families' capacity for economic mobility, but I couldn't have guessed that, as my colleagues and I sought answers to these questions,[1] America itself would change so quickly. I certainly did not anticipate the Great Recession or how much I would learn from its effects on ordinary families' everyday lives. Over the course of our research, we spoke to families whose hopes, dreams, and frustrations were emblematic of those shared by millions of Americans trying to get ahead. We watched as their children matured and, amid a transforming economic climate, their fortunes changed—sometimes for the better but more often for the worse. Some of the young children we met in 1998 grew up to attend elite schools, while others dropped out of high school to toil at low-level service jobs. One was murdered in her home by a stray bullet. Again and again, we saw starry aspirations crash headfirst into the reality of toxic inequality.

Again and again we saw that personal virtues could not ensure positive or improving life outcomes. Those families that successfully passed their status to the next generation often used wealth on multiple occasions to provide head starts and help overcome setbacks. Those families without such resources often could not pass their social status along to their children, who tended to fare poorly. In most cases, such young adults confronted a full spectrum of challenges: weak school systems, fragile communities, a stagnating and stumbling economy, and personal problems, poor health, or family troubles. Without wealth, they often found it nearly impossible to recover from these converging difficulties.

Social institutions and government policies indisputably bend individual life trajectories and tend to lock children into the race and class status of the families they were born into—but that doesn't mean there's no hope for change or that only a few individuals will ever achieve uphill mobility against steep odds. Starting with the lives, challenges, and needs of real families, we can build an agenda for significant reform that can turn the tide against toxic inequality. For toxic inequality is not inevitable or intractable; nor is it unpredictable. It results from the rules and choices that structure America's economy. Since the early 1970s, corporate interests have dominated the writing of these rules, and the result is a weakened economy in which prosperity is hoarded and most families struggle to achieve or maintain a middle-class lifestyle, while a tiny elite amasses an increasing share of the nation's wealth.[2]

In recent decades, the growing power of the very wealthy and of corporations to influence government policies has increasingly shaped the conditions and prospects of families like the ones we interviewed. Changes in patents and other intellectual property rights created monopolies and super-profits for pharmaceutical companies. Corporations and their lobbyists have bent antitrust rules to suit their interests and solidify market control. Corporate lobbying turned labor laws against workers in favor of the bottom line. As a result, the American public pays higher prices for medicine, Internet services, food, airline tickets, and banking services than citizens of other advanced nations. Recent legislation has abated some health, safety, and environmental standards. American workers have fewer leave days and paid holidays as well as fewer benefits than counterparts in advanced economies.[3] It is more difficult to organize a union. Bankruptcy laws have been modified to allow corporations to close down more easily, with fewer obligations to workers and communities. Meanwhile, home owners burdened with mortgage debt and graduates with student debt face years of payments and threats to their credit histories.

Yet, by wedding what we have learned from our family interviews with other social science research, we can map out the kinds of big changes needed to create equitable prosperity. An understanding of how families truly achieve success and sustained mobility and of the roadblocks that throw families too easily off that path will point the way forward from toxic inequality to equity. Family wealth is of fundamental importance to economic mobility and well-being, and any serious agenda for change must have at its core wealth-building for those who need it the most.

For instance, there must be a robust portfolio shift in public investment for public goods through a transformed tax code. Currently the tax code subsidizes wealth accumulation and preservation for the wealthiest. More than $400 billion goes annually to incentivize individual wealth, with 53 percent of the individual wealth-creating benefits given to the wealthiest 5 percent, while the "bottom 60" percent of the population receives a meager 4 percent of the total. Instead, the savings and investment incentives embedded in the US tax code should bolster the households of modest means that need them the most. We need not abolish all tax expenditures or create huge, costly new programs. We simply need to redirect existing public investments to those for whom support will make the intended public good concrete and reachable. The results would be a deeper prosperity, improved family well-being, and perhaps another great leap forward for democracy—on par with some of the great, successful wealth-building policies of our past.

At their best, these grand policies of the past—for instance, those put in place by the Homestead, National Housing, and Social Security acts—were largely effective in bringing the sought-after public good to fruition. At the same time, however, these and similar policies were profoundly racist in design or execution and most certainly in outcome. Along with our tragic past from slavery to Jim Crow, they created and solidified the foundations of today's racial wealth gap in the United States. For example, Social Security originally excluded agricultural and domestic workers, jobs with heavy concentrations of blacks and Latinos, locking them out of the nation's basic retirement system for several decades. Two-thirds of those barred from Social Security were blacks. According to one estimate, $158 billion (in 2016 dollars) in benefits would have gone to blacks and other nonwhites had the Social Security system been inclusive from the beginning.[4] Thus, moving forward in a purely color-blind fashion with bluntly universal policies is inadequate and will only sediment racial inequality deeper into American society. Instead, any agenda for change must recognize that the means of achieving shared public goods will differ according to context and constituency. Creating inclusive retirement security for all, for instance, requires targeting the populations and communities that lack access to structured accounts at their workplaces. Efforts to enhance family prosperity and broad equity must reinforce one another. To do this, we must ask how much every policy proposal, existing policy, and suggestion for institutional reform would do to close the racial wealth gap.

In sum, two principles must anchor an agenda for change for America's families: namely, wealth-building and racial justice. One connects our aspirational, democratic, and American values to public goods. As we have seen, the United States invests hugely in home ownership, retirement security, and education because we believe these goods benefit the largest number of people in the largest possible way while strengthening society. The other principle takes into account the biggest drivers of inequality that propel both historic income and wealth inequality and the widening racial wealth gap, turning them into equity investments.

We must put striving families, their economic security and futures, and equity front and center as our nation moves forward. I am confident that a vast majority of American families share most of the mobility and economic security challenges;[5] at the same time, we should recognize that shared challenges and common goals do not necessarily mean one solution fits all or is appropriate for all constituencies or circumstances.

This chapter shapes an agenda for change. In doing so, it draws not only on my researching and writing about these critical issues but also on my experience as an activist for change in grassroots organizations, state and national coalitions, and local, state, and national policy spheres. Over the years of this study, for example, I was a commissioner on the Massachusetts Asset Development Commission and a member of the Commonwealth of Massachusetts Economic Prosperity Advisory Council, the Tax Alliance for Economic Mobility, the Federal Reserve Bank of Boston's Working Group on Reducing Racial Wealth Inequality, and the National Closing the Racial Wealth Gap Initiative. I have heard from residents and community organizations across the country in places like East St. Louis about how the racial wealth gap plays out in their locales, and I've joined a working dinner with the secretary of the Treasury to discuss housing finance reform options in the wake of the foreclosure crisis.

Shaped by these experiences, the policies discussed here echo great ideas from many sources. In most cases, I will detail the key features of policies needed for change, leaving the precise design and mechanisms and the tactical work of actually executing change to advocates, policymakers, and politicians. I will highlight proven policies and tools already at our disposal and recommend new ones that would place more families on the road to prosperity. Details matter, of course, and no policy proposal should pass muster unless it actually improves well-being, equity, and racial justice for the many people who have lived so long without them.

Previous chapters have detailed how even universal-appearing policies have fostered wealth-generating opportunities in white communities while excluding families of color. Social Security, the Federal Housing Administration (FHA) programs, and the GI Bill created opportunities for many World War II veterans and helped an entire generation of white families build wealth through home ownership and higher education; overwhelmingly, however, these advantages did not extend to families of color. FHA became the foundation of residential segregation after World War II. Some policies were racist in design and execution; others were well intentioned but benefitted whites disproportionately by largely excluding families of color. Even today, public school financing and housing policies that are racially neutral on their face reinforce patterns of segregation established years ago, leading to very real and negative consequences for school quality and for home equity values in communities of color.

Given these realities and that burgeoning wealth inequality and the widening racial wealth gap have common drivers, policymakers and analysts must consider how a broad array of policies—from those targeting family finances, such as tax incentives and savings matches, to wider-ranging ones in such areas as education or housing—impact family wealth. And the policy design process must candidly incorporate the goal of racial equity. We need to know how any prospective policy might affect family savings and family wealth by race and ethnicity. Applying such a racial justice filter to both new and existing policies can ensure that they foster equitable wealth building in communities of color, both avoiding past policy errors and countering ongoing, often hidden discrimination.

How might this work? The Institute on Assets and Social Policy (IASP), working with the public policy organization Dēmos, has created a policy analysis framework, the Racial Wealth Audit (RWA), to examine and measure how a particular policy might generate wealth and for whom. Using national data on household wealth, the RWA assesses the distributional consequences of a particular policy by race and ethnicity, highlighting the expected changes to median wealth among white families and families of color. This specific focus on the policy's impact by race and ethnicity will help avoid seemingly positive policies that may increase family wealth in general but have distorted effects across communities and worsen wealth disparities.

To see how the RWA operates, consider the example of the US Treasury Department's late 2015 launch of myRA retirement savings accounts. Two in five workers without a retirement account have jobs that do not offer one, and more than three in five part-time workers do not have employer-backed accounts. The policy innovation, designed and implemented by Treasury, thus aimed to boost retirement savings among workers, particularly those without access to plans offered by employers, almost as starter plans. Households with incomes below $131,000 ($193,000 for couples) are eligible and can save up to $15,000 in these new myRA accounts. Contributions can be taken directly from pay-checks, bank accounts, or tax refunds. Workers contribute money after income taxes are paid, and any investment gains and withdrawals are then tax-free. To assess this policy's potential, IASP focused just on households in the thirty-five-to-sixty-four age group, those families most likely to be saving for retirement, and assumed that everybody in the targeted population would participate and reach the maximum savings amount, $15,000. Both of these assumptions are unrealistic in practice, but they help to reveal the maximum feasible benefit. Given the policy target of reaching workers without access to retirement accounts through their jobs and who meet eligibility criteria, the RWA revealed that 30.6 percent of white families, 48.1 percent of African American families, and 70.2 percent of Latino families are eligible for myRA accounts, suggesting that myRA is a means toward a common, universal goal that takes account of different groups' particular situations—and, specifically, of the heavy concentration of workers of color in firms and sectors of the economy, especially in the private sector, whose employers do not offer workplace-based access to retirement savings. And RWA modeling, again assuming maximum participation, further revealed that the retirement account alone could reduce the black-white wealth gap at the median (that is, in the fiftieth percentile) by $7,000, or 4.6 percent for this age group; the white-Latino gap would close by $10,100, or 6.9 percent. Changes at lower wealth levels would be even more robust. In the twenty-fifth wealth percentile, myRAs could close the white-black wealth gap by 23.2 percent, or $7,890, and the white-Latino gap by 23.8 percent, or $7,410. RWA analysis demonstrated, then, that myRA would build wealth for all who are eligible while adding wealth disproportionately to more working families of color.[6]

We must keep several final points in mind regarding an ambitious reform agenda. First, any universal, race-blind policy will be inadequate to correct the persisting legacies of centuries of discriminatory policy. Indeed, the word "universal" itself warrants rethinking. When a policymaker or politician calls a process or policy universal, we generally take this to mean that everybody is equally eligible. Instead of seeking universal *eligibility*, however, we should pursue universal *goals*. Once we have defined the universal goal, whether it's early childhood development, pre-K education, housing stability, higher education, quality health care, or a secure and dignified retirement, then we must recognize the need for a variety of strategies or means to move families and communities in different situations toward this outcome. The myRA is one example of such targeted universalism.[7] While providing benefits to those eligible, this approach disproportionately touches the most disadvantaged and provides results most likely to enhance retirement security and close the racial wealth gap.

The second consideration is affordability. Politicians and conservative commentators have taught many Americans to throw up their hands and say the nation cannot afford the policies needed to produce a more equitable society. That is false. We choose how we spend, and we spend over $600 billion on the military and $400 billion on individual wealth-generating provisions in the current tax code. Currently, public investments for public goods, especially the mortgage interest deduction and tax expenditures related to retirement savings, overwhelmingly favor the wealthy. Regarding tax expenditures, as a nation we need merely rebalance our portfolio of public investments; carrying out a truly transformative, equitable, and prosperity-building policy agenda would require no new net tax expenditures. Resourcing new mobility and equity policy strategies, however, will necessitate new investments. When feasible, I will indicate the approximate costs of new policies and suggest how to pay for them. The ultimate question, however, is which investments best accord with our values. We owe it to ourselves as Americans to choose investments that match our democratic aspirations.

Third, we must distinguish between policies that improve individuals' or families' economic mobility and those that push in the direction of greater equity. For example, a proven program like Family Self-Sufficiency (FSS) greatly assists participating families in moving from subsidized rents and poor neighborhoods to more stable communities, housing security, and possibly home ownership. Witness Patricia Arrora's journey. However, FSS does little to narrow wealth inequality or the racial wealth gap because the program lacks the scale necessary to include all eligible families. Similarly, a children's savings account (CSA) is crucial to putting young people on the road to college enrollment and completion and a brighter future. However, in the context of rising college costs and debt, CSAs by themselves will not do much to reduce wealth inequality; nor will they close the racial wealth gap. Family economic mobility is important, and as mobility strategies, both FSS and CSAs are vital. For this reason the policy agenda in this chapter includes them and similar programs. However, we must never lose sight of the need to narrow our wealth divides—and mobility policies alone cannot do this work.

Fourth, ambitious policy innovations should be future-proof, at least to some extent. To maximize its chances of success, or even to allow it to operate long enough to learn if it works effectively or to gather enough information to know how to improve it, a policy cannot be at the mercy of changing political winds and shifting fortunes. Changes in the tax code, for instance, are more difficult to reverse than partisan congressional legislation and often persevere for decades; legislation with some bipartisan buy-in is more enduring.

Finally, what I call policy articulation is critical. As reforms or new investments are made in one area, we must protect other interconnected parts of the system to ensure that new resources actually add to existing supports. For instance, when it comes to CSAs for higher education (discussed later in this chapter), policy articulation would require some measures that protect against new tuition increases simply because universities and state legislators anticipate young college applicants with new access to small pots of gold.

A tentative, piecemeal, or fragmentary response will not suffice to create equity and family prosperity; instead, we must take bold steps and enact multiple, interconnected policies to transform America. As the families highlighted in this book suggest, any agenda for change must strengthen housing and community stability for families, emphasize quality jobs with higher wages and benefits, ensure retirement security, provide quality education, encourage savings, and reform tax policy to foster both equity and mobility.

Strengthen Housing and Community Stability for Families

Patricia Arrora's home was underwater; Rachel and Shawn Andrews' was located in a weak and disinvested neighborhood; the Medinas' was in a community rapidly transitioning from home owners to renters and absentee landowners. Linda Diamond's daughter was killed by a stray bullet in a neighborhood where gunshots are commonplace, Cindy Breslin's rent far outpaced her social assistance and rental subsidy, and Michelle Johnson's family home was in foreclosure. Lindsay Bonde needed new housing because she could no longer climb stairs. Meanwhile, the Ackermans' home increased in value and withstood the ravages of the Great Recession and housing crisis; the Clark and Mills families, with the help of parental support, owned homes in middle-class communities; and Reese Otis had a home on the island where she grew up.

Home equity and community stability remain key components of wealth acquisition and growth for most Americans. Both are more accessible to whites than to people of color. Tellingly, of the seven families we interviewed between 2010 and 2012 that had been threatened with foreclosure, were already in foreclosure proceedings, or had been foreclosed upon, six were African American. This tracks national data that the housing meltdown, predatory lending, actual foreclosures, and the resulting tremendous destruction of wealth hit communities of color hardest.[8]

Ensuring housing stability, then, must be a centerpiece of transformative policy. We must first stop the harm of impending foreclosure by means of principal reductions and loan modifications through Fannie Mae and Freddie Mac, the government-sponsored enterprises that buy mortgages on the secondary market, pool them, and sell them as mortgage-backed securities to investors on the open market. The government's Home Affordable Modification Program, for example, reduced mortgage payments by adjusting interest rates, extending loan terms, and reducing or forbearing principal. This program, however, is set to expire at the end of 2016. Reinstating it would ensure an important tool for ending the lingering harms of the 2008 crisis.

Tax benefits to support home ownership—including deductions for mortgage interest and property taxes—are the largest individual tax expenditures, but they primarily subsidize wealthier households. Only one out of four taxpayers claims the home mortgage interest deduction, and of households that take it, the greatest subsidy goes to the wealthiest households because the higher the filer's tax bracket, the greater the value of the deduction; and the larger the home—and loan—the greater the amount of mortgage interest eligible for deduction. The Tax Alliance for Economic Mobility has outlined several approaches to redirect mortgage interest deduction benefits so as to allow lower-income households and households of color more capacity to purchase a first home and build home equity.[9] One is to reform the mortgage interest deduction itself, capping the deductible amount of mortgage interest or turning the deduction

into a credit. As only 11 percent of filers with incomes under $40,000 itemize deductions, the vast majority of lower-
income families could potentially benefit if the deduction
were a credit instead.

Another approach would be to adjust the portfolio of
public investments and pivot to tax benefits that encourage wealth-building through home ownership among lower-
income families. Some options include a first-time home
buyer's credit, a refundable tax credit for property taxes paid,
and an annual flat tax credit for home owners. Each would
cap the home mortgage interest deduction at 15 percent, repeal the property tax deduction, and retain the existing tax
treatment of capital gains on owner-occupied housing. For
people who sold their home, the first $500,000 of financial
gain would be exempted (for a couple), and anything over
that amount would be subject to a 14 percent capital gains
tax rate.[10] A version of the first-time home-buyer tax credit
was implemented during the Great Recession and phased
out after 2010. A new, refundable version of this credit
would allow low- and moderate-income first-time home
buyers access to home ownership. As in previous versions,
the maximum credit would be $7,500, and it would have
an income phaseout ($150,000 to 170,000 for joint filers).[11]
Such features would ensure that it targeted the American
families most in need of affordable housing. While some of
the ideas under discussion represent different paths, many
can work together.

An even more ambitious proposal calls for a twenty-
first-century Homestead Act. This would create a govern-

ment-backed, preferred-rate, thirty-year fixed mortgage, with preference given to families—as opposed to speculative investors—purchasing homes foreclosed due to proven mortgage fraud. It would also provide home-improvement loans targeted to families who purchase foreclosed homes in areas stricken by the mortgage crisis or in disinvested communities, like those in which the Andrewses and the Medinas lived. This would augur a far better future than one where financial speculators like the Blackstone Group and the Lone Star Funds continue to buy distressed and foreclosed properties and bundle them together for absentee landlord-investors.

Housing stability involves both home ownership and renting, and federal policy should address the latter as well. Indeed, the mortgage crisis led to highly restrictive lending by financial institutions; as a result home ownership rates have been falling since the mid-2000s, and rents are increasing faster than incomes. A federal renters' tax credit, administered by states, would augment renters' stability. Each state would receive a fixed dollar amount of credits allocated for renters and for developing affordable housing. The state of Massachusetts, for instance, already has a proven and effective renter's tax deduction. Renters are eligible for a deduction of up to 50 percent of rent paid for a principal residence, up to $3,000 annually. This deduction gives Massachusetts renters access to some of the supports that home owners receive, though they still lag far behind. A national version of this deduction would go a long way to making rental housing more affordable. Policy articulation would ensure that rules are in place to prevent rapacious landlords from simply scooping up the tax credit by raising rents.

Finally, we must do more to end racial segregation in housing. The 1968 Fair Housing Act promoted real progress; yet place of residence persists as a strong predictor of success and life chances. Residential segregation remains high, and racially concentrated areas of poverty exist in virtually every metropolitan area, with high costs in the form of weak and declining infrastructures and services for families living in those locales. Racial discrimination continues to steer families into residentially segregated communities. No new laws are needed to end discriminatory practices; simply updating and rigorously enforcing existing laws would be sufficient. The Fair Housing Act tops the list of housing nondiscrimination laws needing strengthening and enforcement; others include Title VI of the Civil Rights Act of 1964, Section 504 of the Rehabilitation Act of 1973, Section 109 of Title I of the Housing and Community Development Act of 1974, Title II of the Americans with Disabilities Act of 1990, and the Architectural Barriers Act of 1968.

Passing a law is very different from enforcing it. We need enforcement of existing fair housing laws because discrimination persists in housing markets. The US Department of Housing and Urban Development (HUD) issued a ruling in July 2015 based on a mountain of research documenting discrimination against minorities at every stage in real estate transactions—in the search for, purchase, and rental of homes, in the assessment of closing costs on loans, and in steering minorities into segregated neighborhoods.[12] Discrimination results in higher housing costs in terms of rents, purchase prices, and mortgage terms. Nearly fifty years after landmark legislation, researchers still found that realtors' marketing efforts increase with house price for white customers but not for black customers, and black customers are more likely to experience steering. The houses that agents show are more likely to deviate from the initial request when the customer is black as opposed to white. Minority home seekers hear about and see fewer homes and apartments than whites, raising the costs of housing searches and limiting choices. African Americans and Hispanics pay higher closing costs than whites with equivalent credit scores and loan amounts. The HUD summary reinforces uncontested social science findings on a significant link between race and the value of home ownership. These findings are consistent with discrimination on the part of real estate agents and financial institutions that results in restricted housing choices for minorities and vastly diminished home equity prospects.

Systemic discrimination is not limited to home ownership and extends deep into rental housing. Regardless of structure and neighborhood characteristics, African Americans experience discrimination, which increases as neighborhoods reach a "tipping point" (from 5 to 20 percent minority share of the community). Segregation persists and maliciously parcels opportunities in the context of toxic inequality, where better-off communities hoard resources and the advantages they transmit. That is why the Orinda Union School District in California persecuted Vivian and her family for daring to attend a public school in a community in which they could not afford to live.

Residential segregation bakes inequality into the lives of families by reproducing parents' disadvantages for their children. Significantly, these involuntary harms are not intractable; we can reverse them. Major recent studies, for example, document substantial improvement in family incomes and lasting educational attainments for children whose families move away from high-poverty neighborhoods and live in lower-poverty ones for several years.[13]

Create Quality Jobs with Higher Wages and Benefits

Employment fragility for some, alongside quality jobs with benefits for others, is at the heart of rising inequality and the racial wealth gap. The experiences of the Medinas, the Barzaks, and even the Ackermans illuminate how underemployment, frequent and extended spells of joblessness, and lower wages significantly reduce families' capacity to generate wealth or even to put enough aside for emergencies and tough times. We need bold and transformative policy to change the current direction of the economy so as to address these inequities.

Full employment ought to be a goal. Currently, monetary policy protects big financial institutions against inflation risks at the expense of prioritizing full employment. Additionally, we need public investment to make the United States a world leader in innovation and modern manufacturing, thus creating a foundation for long-term job growth. Such investment would build better roads and bridges, expand public transit options, provide access to the digital economy through the Internet, produce advanced aviation technology and modern airports, develop a world-class high-speed passenger rail system, and construct a twenty-first-century energy infrastructure. These improvements will not be cheap, with a likely price tag in the range of $50 billion a year for five years. They are, however, essential not only to our ability to compete globally but also to Americans' well-being and safety. The cost of doing nothing is exorbitant.

The revelation in early 2016 that Flint, Michigan's water supply had delivered poisonous levels of lead mostly to low-income, minority neighborhoods represents the tip of the iceberg, a warning of imminent dangers posed by our decaying infrastructure. A major infrastructure investment would open up job and subcontracting opportunities to communities denied them in the past, and expanding public transportation would promote equal access to jobs and opportunities long after infrastructure projects were completed.

Alongside ambitious new investments to create jobs, other reforms would expand the employment capital provided by new and existing jobs. A significant portion of the private sector has shifted from defined benefit pension plans to defined contribution or cash balance plans. As states face high funding deficits for their state and local pensions, public pension systems are also shifting away from defined benefit plans. Despite these shifts, defined benefit plans are more effective at ensuring individuals have retirement security, because they offer higher benefits and deliver payments almost exclusively through annuities. Federal guarantees should protect current and future defined benefit pension holders, particularly those who work in the public sector. An agency like the Pensions Benefit Guaranty Corporation, which insures pension plans for the private sector, could do the same for public defined benefit and cash balance plans. Such an entity could also strengthen the funding requirements and expand this regulation to state and local public plans. While states must understandably implement innovative strategies to decrease actuarial deficits, they cannot implement such reforms on the backs of individuals in or near retirement or lower-paid workers.

Additionally, the federal government should strengthen the right to bargain by easing legal barriers to unionization, imposing stricter penalties on illegal antiunion intimidation tactics, and amending laws to reflect the changing workplace. Corporate practices in the twenty-first-century global economy—from growing reliance on a contingent workforce, to keeping work hours just below minimum requirements for benefits and Affordable Care Act coverage, to releasing workers and rehiring them as so-called subcontractors, to imposing just-in-time work scheduling, to outsourcing, to offshore avoidance of income taxes, to wage theft—are squeezing working people in new ways. Unions can attend to some of these issues, but government needs to set the standards by attaching strong pro-worker stipulations to its contracts and development subsidies, increasing funding for enforcement, and raising penalties for violating labor standards.

A living wage should be the goal; building to that by raising the minimum wage is a good interim step forward. Minimum-wage campaigns, like that for $15 an hour, are increasingly popular and successful in city and state initiatives. Given what we know about the racial and gender bias in who has access to employment-based benefits, living- and minimum-wage initiatives must combine wealth-protecting and -escalating benefit structures (paid sick leave, retirement, medical, and dental) with the bare bones of hourly wages.

Together these ideas for full employment, infrastructure improvement, pension reform, workers' rights, and a living wage would build wealth and reduce the racial wealth gap significantly. A more ambitious reform—a federal job guarantee—could have even more impact. This ambitious reform would entitle people looking for jobs or with less than thirty-five hours per week of paid employment to perform work of public benefit at an enhanced minimum wage. This would replace unemployment and underemployment with paid employment for up to thirty-five hours per week. A federal job guarantee is a sure path to full employment and could be pegged to stronger workers' rights in conjunction with public infrastructure projects. Some of these approaches overlap, but taken together they would transform the workplace from a site of inequality into one of equity and racial justice.

Policy affords formal paths for opportunity, access, and inclusion, but informal employer and workplace discrimination persists to erode gains, block pathways, and undermine policy success. Evidence abounds detailing that discrimination in employment is far from a thing of the past and remains deeply embedded today. It is so strong that a white applicant with a criminal record is just as likely as a black person with no criminal history, if not more so, to get a callback or job interview. This drives home just how much race matters in employment, "with being black viewed as tantamount to being a convicted felon."[14] Another study underscores the deep entrenchment of implicit bias; "job applicants with African American–sounding names get far fewer callbacks for each resume they send out."[15] Further, the study found, it is hard to overcome this hurdle in job callbacks because improving credentials and social skills did not necessarily overcome discrimination in getting callbacks for job interviews.

We must also firmly enforce existing laws and policies regarding employer discrimination. Good laws on the books already include Title VII of the Civil Rights Act of 1964, which prohibits employment discrimination based on race, color, religion, sex, or national origin; the Equal Pay Act of 1963, which protects against sex-based wage discrimination; the Age Discrimination in Employment Act of 1967, which protects individuals age forty and older; Titles I and V of the Americans with Disabilities Act of 1990, which prohibit employment discrimination against persons with disabilities; Sections 501 and 505 of the Rehabilitation Act of 1973, which prohibit discrimination against qualified individuals with disabilities who work in the federal government; and the Civil Rights Act of 1991, which provides monetary damages in cases of intentional employment discrimination.

Fair housing and employment laws reveal some important lessons. Persistent bias undermines the best of intentions; and although good laws exist, their effectiveness depends upon rigorous enforcement. We cannot attend only to the formal policy arena but must address informal bias as well.

Ensure Retirement Security

While the Arrora, Andrews, and Medina families' stories suggest the challenges of preparing for a secure retirement, the Ackerman family offers a model of what strong, employer-based benefits comprise. The Ackermans' benefits included a matched retirement savings plan in which the employee is enrolled by default. While these ample benefits sometimes appear in public and nonprofit employment sectors (e.g., private universities), one should not be fooled into thinking that offering them is a private, virtuous, or voluntary choice on employers' part, because a robust system of public investment subsidizes these benefits. We need federal and state incentives to encourage all businesses, up to a reasonable minimum of employees, to offer retirement plans, and we should reapportion the current public investment to extend tax benefits to larger portions of the workplace.

Most Americans rely on Social Security as their main source of income during retirement, but this relatively modest program is inadequate on its own and needs strengthening. Social Security is the bedrock of retirement security for most low- and moderate-income families, and its disability and survivor protections are especially important for those who depend on them to cover the largest share of their living expenses. We should increase Social Security benefits with a focus on economically insecure beneficiaries who do not have the necessary savings or income to get by in retirement or in the event of a family member's disability or early death. The Commission to Modernize Social Security, for instance, developed a plan to extend Social Security's solvency while improving benefits for the vulnerable.[16] The plan would, among other things, raise revenue by lifting the cap on wages taxed, flattening benefits for high earners, and gradually increasing the payroll tax by 1 percent over twenty years, while expanding benefits for the very old and those with very low incomes. Additionally, the plan reinstates Social Security survivor benefits for students over the age of eighteen attending college and provides credits for workers who take time out of the paid workforce for caregiving purposes. Indeed, for a more thorough option, we could eliminate entirely the cap on wages subject to the Social Security payroll tax— $118,500 was the limit in 2015—to extend the solvency of Social Security and make the necessary adjustments that will ensure it better meets the needs of the nation's most vulnerable citizens.

The 2016 recommendations of the Bipartisan Policy Center's Commission on Retirement Security and Personal Savings also aimed to improve benefits for those most likely to be financially insecure. These recommendations include an attempt to make the benefit formula more progressive, a basic minimum benefit designed to be more effective than the existing special minimum benefit, an enhanced elderly survivors' benefit, and the continuation of survivors' benefits for students through age twenty-two. These benefit improvements are very much needed. Social Security won't have sufficient revenue from payroll and other Social Security taxes to cover full benefits for program participants after 2034. The report also includes several measures to restore the program's long-term solvency by gradually raising the payroll tax and raising the maximum cap. But it also shortchanged some of the most vulnerable workers with a revised benefit formula and raised the age for receiving full retirement benefits.[17]

Due to the wide and persistent racial wealth gap, communities of color experience economically perilous retirement years. Beyond strengthening Social Security, we need to take several steps to create a retirement future that is secure for all. Establishing universal matched retirement accounts is one.

Low-income families, communities of color in particular, are less likely to have access to workplace retirement plans than the general population. Many don't have enough money saved to meet a minimum for opening an investment account on their own. As a result, millions of workers in America lack options to save for retirement. To supplement employer-based benefits, universal retirement accounts, under federal oversight, should be established and workers automatically enrolled with an opt-out option. Ideally, these accounts should have a federal component matching a percentage of annual income up to $1,000 for low- and moderate-income workers.

Earlier we saw how the US Treasury developed myRA accounts to address some of these common barriers to retirement saving and to provide a simple, safe, and affordable option for working people. Working people can open a myRA account with no start-up cost and pay no fees for its maintenance; myRA has no minimum contribution requirement, so savers can contribute the amount that best fits their budget. The Treasury backs the investment, and the myRA carries no risk of losing money. Future strengthening of myRA should expand it by raising the $15,000 limit and enabling other similar simple options in order to increase access to tax-preferred retirement savings accounts.

The federal government is not the only place where retirement reform is percolating. States are taking similar policy action to provide simple and accessible ways to begin planning for retirement. They could follow the progressive lead of Illinois and California, which are launching workplace-based retirement plans designed for working people not offered access to plans at their places of employment.

Provide Quality Education

The five-year-olds we first met in 1998 are by now on divergent pathways to adulthood, and their experiences in educational systems helped to shape their vastly differing life chances. The stories of St. Louis youngsters Peter Ackerman and Tina Medina capture this clearly. We must improve higher education prospects for people like Tina, ensure that middle-class young adults like Andy Mills can pay for college, and improve the disinvested, frail, and vulnerable school systems that failed Keneysha Breslin and Desi Johnson. Education is a critical public good and, once acquired, a key individual asset, one of the most pivotal resources for family economic security. But great disparities remain in access to education and educational quality in America. We must strengthen the entire spectrum from prekindergarten to higher education.

Universal pre-K is a crucial tool for reducing poverty and improving subsequent educational and economic outcomes, particularly among vulnerable youth. There is good evidence that early childhood education could help eliminate the achievement gap between socioeconomic groups. A 2013 study of low-income children randomly assigned to a two-year, center-based early childhood education intervention found that it significantly boosted their school readiness. These effects remain substantial for several years of early schooling. States should create, with federal support provided in the form of revenue and subsidies, pre-K educational systems and thereby provide every young child with quality, publicly funded preschool.

Today, the majority of high-paying jobs demand education beyond a high school diploma, especially those requiring science, technology, engineering, or math degrees. These account for more than 10 percent of jobs in the United States, and many of them pay wages close to double the US average. Yet the United States has one of the highest high school dropout rates among industrialized nations and ranks low in college attainment. This national challenge is accompanied by a severe achievement gap between white students and students of color, who disproportionately attend schools with fewer resources and poorer educational quality. Leveling educational disparities requires adequate resource allocation, including equitable state financing for schools and districts as well as improved support for and distribution of highly qualified and effective teachers and principals. Property taxes are the primary sources of local funding for public schools, meaning that richer districts have greater capacity to provide quality education and poorer districts are continually strapped for resources—even as children there start school further behind and arrive at school with more health conditions and learning challenges. A few states try to ameliorate this disparity by using formulas to reapportion this common resource, and more should do so. Equitable formulas will not be a magic solution to school achievement inequality, but they will go a long way to making resources and chances for success more equitable.

Stephanie Andrews grew up in a chancy St. Louis neighborhood, but rather than choosing to pay for private schooling, her parents enrolled her in a great magnet school that kept her somewhat close to home and in the public school system. But schools like Stephanie's are too rare, and lacking similar resources, the other public schools around her were very weak. More equitable distribution of resources could ensure that vulnerable communities have access to magnet schools that prepare students for careers of the future—focusing, for example, on entrepreneurship, business, technology, creative arts, social media and communications, and health care—and use digital learning platforms and strategies.

Beyond secondary school, tuition costs that outpace inflation at a time of stagnant or reduced family income endanger college access and completion. Policymakers must champion affordable and equitable access to higher education, and tuition increases at public and private universities must be held to the rate of inflation to limit the financial burden on students. Attaching federal aid, tax subsidies, and research grants to tuition-control measures is one way to accomplish this. The larger issue, however, is the reduction of investment in public higher education. The cutbacks have come largely at the state level. In the face of the multiyear, nationwide fiscal crisis, many states have reduced financing for public universities, cut back on enrollment and university resources, and increased tuition and fees to compensate. These public spending cuts and private revenue increases have diminished higher education access and quality without addressing the need to reduce universities' internal inefficiencies. At the federal level, Pell Grants must be reinvigorated so that they serve their intended purpose of adequately supporting college attendance and completion among low- and moderate-income students. The alternative is even higher student debt and an even wider college-completion divide between young adults from rich and poor families.

And in response to heavy and increasingly unsustainable student loan debt, policymakers should expand early debt-assistance programs that allow graduates to cap federal loan payments at a percentage of their monthly income. Further-more, opportunities for graduate debt forgiveness and loan modifications to reduce debt should be expanded. Dēmos and IASP have proposed ways to achieve the double bottom line of reducing student debt in a way that closes the racial wealth gap.[18] One proposal, for instance, would eliminate stu-dent debt for households making $50,000 or below, and this step would reduce the racial wealth gap between black and white families at the median by nearly 7 percent. The effects of doing so would be far greater among households in the twenty-fifth percentile of wealth, where it would reduce the black-white wealth disparity by nearly 37 percent. Among such low-wealth households, eliminating debt for just those making $25,000 or less reduces the black-white wealth gap by over 50 percent.[19]

Tax expenditures are another area for reform when it comes to education. The American Opportunity Tax Credit (AOTC) is a credit for qualified education expenses paid for an eligible student for the first four years of higher education, created in 2009 as part of the economic recovery package. More low- and moderate-income households qualify for the maximum annual credit of $2,500 per eligible student than for higher education tax subsidies like the Lifetime Learning Credit. AOTC is more accessible because it is a partially refundable credit, meaning that if the credit brings the amount of tax owed to zero, 40 percent of any remaining amount of the credit (up to $1,000) can be refunded. Expanding the refundable portion of the AOTC would help to broaden access to lower-income households. Other reforms could increase access to the AOTC by allowing low- and moderate-income families to access the credit before they are required to pay for higher education expenses. The bipartisan tax deal at the end of 2015 made AOTC permanent.

Build Savings from Birth

Over 1.3 million American children—and more than half of minority children—are born each year into families with negligible savings to invest in their futures. Yet research indicates that lower-income children whose families have even moderate savings are more likely to be invested in their futures and succeed in life. Savings can offer another way to ensure wider access to higher education, for instance. Children in low- and moderate-income families with college savings of just $500 are three times more likely to enroll in college and four times more likely to graduate.[20] And promoting college attendance and completion—and the accompanying increased lifetime income and economic mobility—is just one way that policies to encourage savings can help to build family wealth over generations.

Children's savings accounts are one tool for accomplishing this. CSAs are based on the simple idea that all families, given the right support, will save and invest in the talents and aspirations of their children. The ideal federal CSA policy would create lifelong, asset-building savings accounts at birth for every child, with more incentives for those that need them the most. These accounts would support savings for higher education, home ownership, retirement, and other mobility-enhancing purposes. This is the aim of the ASPIRE Act, repeatedly introduced in Congress with bipartisan support since 2005. The act would create an account for all children at birth, seeded with $500, plus an additional deposit for children of low-income parents.

Policymakers should also reform federal 529 accounts, tax-benefitted college savings accounts created through federal policy and offered by the states. The accounts offer a universal savings platform, and all states have at least one plan. However, at present, lower-income households receive few benefits: those in the bottom half of the income distribution own less than 2 percent of all savings in these accounts. Federal legislation could facilitate, encourage, and subsidize more inclusive 529 plans in the states. Many states are already working to increase participation among lower-income populations through lower fees, matched savings, and outreach. The state-level experiments that are succeeding in increasing college savings among lower-income residents should inform changes to federal 529 policy.

Most ambitious would be a "baby bonds" trust program to mitigate intergenerational barriers to wealth accumulation for low-income families and people of color. In 2005, the Labour government in the United Kingdom implemented a program of baby bonds, the Child Trust Fund, creating endowed trusts for children at birth in amounts ranging from £250 to £500 depending on existing family resources. But created by administrative fiat, the program was summarily ended in 2011 when a new coalition government took office. In the United States, a more robust and future-proof, or sustainable, version of this program might endow children with a trust at birth that would increase progressively until they reached eighteen. Depending on the initial investment and future contributions, the accounts would reach $30,000 to $60,000 for those born into households in the lowest wealth quartile.[21] An attractive feature of this endowment is the potential for private, family, community, and philanthropic participation. The federal government should provide these accounts for every child. Federal funds should seed each account, with larger deposits for infants in low-income families with minimal savings. At age eighteen, a young person could use the money for tuition or training, to start a business, or to buy a home.

IASP analysis of this ambitious policy suggests it could have a profound effect both on wealth accumulation and on the racial wealth gap among young adult households. Depending on funding and participation, these accounts could reduce the racial wealth gap by about 20 to 80 percent, while raising the wealth levels of all groups. An early 2016 report from the Annie E. Casey Foundation documented how implementation of baby bonds a generation ago would have entirely wiped out the black-white and Latino-white wealth gaps for all eighteen- to thirty-four-year-olds.[22] It's misleading to simply tally costs. While initially costing approximately $21 billion, this investment in children could reduce dependence on public benefits, increase consumer buying power, boost investment in businesses and homes, and move our country to greater equity.

Reform Tax Policy

Tax policy affected every family highlighted in this book, as it does just about every family in America. Mortgage interest deductions, retirement savings tax expenditures, and Earned Income Tax Credit (EITC) refunds are just a few ways that tax policy intersects with families' experiences in their homes and communities, with work and retirement. This chapter has already focused on some sensible ways to transform the mortgage interest deduction and tax mechanisms around retirement savings so as to better reach those families most in need, as opposed to largely advantaging those who are already wealthy. The EITC is a rare example of tax policy that provides major support for low- and moderate-income working people. Depending upon marital status, working families with children and incomes below $39,000 to $53,000 may be eligible for EITC. Those workers without children and with incomes below about $15,000 are also eligible. EITC is refundable even if the credit is larger than the worker's tax liability. The average 2015 EITC refund was slightly over $3,000 for a family with children and under $300 for families without children. In 2013, 6.2 million more people would have been in poverty without EITC, and more than half of those were children.[23] Twenty-six states supplement the federal credit. Massachusetts, for example, adds another 15 percent on top of the federal EITC.

A proven and effective policy tool like the Earned Income Tax Credit, which lifts more working families out of poverty than anything other than a good wage, should be strengthened. Raising the minimum wage is crucial, but to best serve working families, it and EITC should complement each other. At the end of 2015, two key improvements to EITC that were set to expire were extended through 2017—removal of the marriage penalty and the provision of larger EITC for families with more than two children. We should continue to strengthen EITC by gradually raising income eligibility and increasing the maximum benefit. In addition, more states also should augment EITC, and the twenty-six states that do so already could boost their supplement and broaden eligibility thresholds for the state matching component.

One additional area for reform is the federal estate tax, an enduring feature of the US tax code since 1916. In its present form, it is the clearest symbol of the power of today's superwealthy families to pass along unearned privileges. Very few estates, just 18 in every 10,000, pay any estate taxes. The 2015 exclusion level below which wealth is protected is nine times higher than it was in 1997, and the top tax rate is 37.5 percent lower. In a better world, we would capture far more revenue from the transfer of unearned property and wealth from one generation to the next in order to provide real opportunities for those not born into affluence and who will inherit little money, or none. We could easily finance children's savings accounts and even an ambitious program of baby bonds with a reformed estate tax. In 2016, the first $5.45 million is excluded for an individual, after which the tax rate is 40 percent. A responsible reform might drop the exclusion to $3.5 million or lower ($7 million for couples) while phasing in gradual increases in the rate, say 45 percent for an estate up to $10 million, 50 percent for estates between $10 and $50 million, 55 percent for those above

$50 million, and 65 percent for billionaires. According to one conservative estimate, such a reformed estate tax would raise $30 billion in additional revenues.[24] This would provide more opportunities to younger Americans while cutting back, even if only slightly, on a process that transmits and locks in inequality at birth.

TOXIC INEQUALITY IMPACTS SOME AMERICANS MORE THAN others, but its cumulative effects damage every family and community and harm our nation as a whole. Time and again, our conversations with ordinary people pointed to a spreading toxic inequality syndrome, in which the accumulation of stressful experiences—job loss, protracted unemployment, eviction or foreclosure, prolonged illness, the end of a relationship—overwhelms a family's or community's ability to stay above water. Toxic inequality syndrome is a product of sustained economic hardships, family adversity, frustrated aspirations, and the persisting uncertainties of life in communities with few resources in times when more and more risk has been shifted to families and individuals. Toxic inequality often produces not only material deprivation but also psychological and even biological changes in children, blocking and cementing families' trajectories and poisoning the lifeblood of communities. We must reverse direction.

We can start by doing right by children. Tina Medina should have had higher education in her future, not dead-end service work. Mishaps easily surmounted by wealthier families should not have derailed Keneysha Breslin's dream of becoming a doctor so easily. Desi Johnson deserved a school that could accommodate her Tourette's syndrome and allow her to thrive, rather than abandoning her to the isolation of bullying.

In our interviews, we also heard many inspiring stories and learned of dreams and aspirations more easily attained with the kinds of policy reforms outlined in this chapter. Rachel Andrews's nation, her community, her family, and she herself would be better off if she achieved her dream to "be of service" in the Peace Corps during her retirement. I suspect Patricia will sign up regardless, but realizing her goal of serving others would be less risky if her community were more stable and she could be certain her daughter would complete college and embark on the road to success. "Real freedom" for Reese Otis entails working with indigenous women in southern Chile, even at minimal pay. Though doing well, Reese is concerned about not having enough retirement savings, and she too would benefit from greater certitude and security. Policies discussed in this chapter would bring these women's dreams closer to reality.

Placing people, families, and communities at the core of our values and our policy direction can also make America a better nation. We have seen how extreme wealth inequality and widening racial inequality reinforce one another, forming the bedrock of America's twenty-first-century toxic inequality. The time has come for a reset. None of us can thrive in a nation divided between a small number of people who possess an ever-larger portion of the income and wealth and everyone else increasingly grasping for a declining share and feeling real pain. It tears at the fabric of our society, posing a fundamental problem for democracy and for the well-being of our families, communities, and nation.

Inequality goes far deeper than just income and wealth. It determines who can overcome obstacles: some have them cleared from their path, while others have trouble recovering from even minor mishaps. At its heart, inequality is about access, opportunity, and just rewards. For too long, toxic inequality has defined the landscape of our country, dictating where people live, how they fare, and what futures their children face. Its mechanisms can seem invisible, even inevitable. But they are man-made, forged by history and preserved by policy. Changing them is up to us.

APPENDIX: THE LEVERAGING MOBILITY STUDY

Toxic Inequality draws upon the Leveraging Mobility Study, a unique database of family interviews collected at two points, from 1998 to 1999 and 2010 to 2012. My colleagues and I initially used census tract data to identify residential neighborhoods in the metropolitan areas of Boston, St. Louis, and Los Angeles that fit the demographic characteristics of the communities we wanted to draw interviews from: white and black middle-income and lower-income communities. I selected a few communities within each metropolitan area from which to interview families with young, school-age children.

Our main recruiting strategy was to approach day-care facilities. I drew up a list of these facilities in the target areas and visited them, introducing the study and myself and then asking permission to use their center to inform families about the study and recruit participants. Only one of the ten centers I approached refused to cooperate. After each family interview, we used what is called a snowball sampling method, whereby we asked families to suggest other families with young children in their neighborhood who might also agree to be interviewed. This moved the study sample outside the day-care centers.

Interviews took place in the participant's home or in another place of their choosing and lasted one to three hours each. Each participant reviewed an informed consent form, signed it, and agreed to be interviewed. We promised, to the best of our abilities, not to divulge participants' identities by protecting the data, reporting certain data only in the aggregate, and stripping out personal data such as names, places of employment, and communities of residence. Further, in any subsequent publications or presentations, we would change family names and other possible identifying information, such as job titles, places of work, and street addresses, to maintain their anonymity. Thus the names used in this book are pseudonyms. All participants received an honorarium for their time. The 184 interviews were recorded, transcribed, and organized into a qualitative data-analysis software package and stored on a secured server that limits Institute on Assets and Social Policy (IASP) access.

At baseline, families had children aged between three and ten years old; most were five years old. More than twelve years later, when we conducted the second wave of 137 interviews between 2010 and 2012, these children were at the end of their high school careers or beyond; the parents were between forty and sixty years old and in the latter half of their working lives. The Leveraging Mobility Study team did an amazing job of finding families twelve years later, telling them about the follow-on interviews, and obtaining participation. Because I had not originally anticipated that the study would evolve into another phase, there had been no attempt since the first interviews to maintain contact with or track the sample of families. As the need to understand the wealth/well-being/mobility connections became more urgent during the Great Recession, the opportunity to follow up with our families became the centerpiece of a large research project. Fortunately, a funder stepped forward. The majority lived in the same city or nearby, but a few had moved to other states, where we contacted and interviewed them.

The baseline and follow-up interviews covered information about the children's education histories and the adults' previous and current community or communities of residence, household incomes and expenditures, household wealth and debt, work histories, family financial and nonfinancial assistance received, and reflections about their economic security and decisions they had made related to using their assets.

The Ford Foundation generously funded the Leveraging Mobility Study. Without Kilolo Kijakazi's leadership, vision, and support, the 2010–2012 set of interviews would not have happened. She set this work in the critical context of a national initiative to close the racial wealth gap. Kilolo has my deepest admiration and total appreciation.

Selected characteristics for families in the Leveraging Mobility Study are described in Table A.1.

TABLE A.1 Leveraging Mobility Study: Selected Family Characteristics, 1998–1999 and 2010–2011

	All Families	African American Families	White Families
Number in 1998	183	89	88
Number in 2010	137	67	65
Median Age, 2010	49	48	50
Median Income, 1998	$58,746	$48,106	$80,400
Median Income, 2010	$69,000	$56,000	$84,000
Median Net Financial Assets	$28,050	$167	$81,350
Median Net Wealth	$79,500	$9,750	$289,000
College Education, 2010	60%	50%	72%
Middle Class	73%	70%	75%
Homeowners, 1998	53%	34%	75%
Homeowners, 2010	69%	51%	91%
Unemployment, 1998–2010	38%	39%	37%
Children in College or on Track		32%	47%
Received Inheritance		5%	19%
Received Large Gifts		39%	56%
Debt over $900 (excluding mortgage)		34%	24%

Figures in 2010 Dollars

ACKNOWLEDGMENTS

I HAVE NOT DONE THIS ALONE. MY GREATEST ASSET IS THE people around me and my partnerships. I stand on broad and strong shoulders. I am grateful to my friends, colleagues, and editors, who were instrumental in all phases of this project. In many ways this book reflects the efforts of many partnerships and teams over the past decade. This solitary book-writing venture puts ideas worked out together into words. I appear as the sole author where dozens could also be listed on the cover.

It's a singular and humbling honor to direct the Institute on Assets and Social Policy. Hannah Thomas, Janet Boguslaw, Tatjana Meschede, Sandy Venner, Alexis Mann, Sara Chaganti, Faith Paul, Becca Loya, Jessica Santos, Charity Adams, and Laura Sullivan were Team One throughout this entire project and represent the collective "we" and "I" in the text. Many ideas were developed in the team process of our research and production of dozens of papers and briefs.

The reader sees the presentation; discovery involved a fully engaged team. Virtually every use of the word "I" in the text should really be "we," because the pronoun refers to various sets of partners and teams. I read interview transcripts many times, listened to the audio recordings, supervised the coding, and visited many of the interview and neighborhood locations. But I did not conduct the interviews; four fabulous and talented members of the Leveraging Mobility Project team did. Hannah Thomas led the Boston team, which included Amy Booxbaum; Robin Moore-Chambers anchored the St. Louis interviewers, which included Sarah Myers, Tanya Perry, and Kenneth Cattage; in Los Angeles Chinyere Usuji acted as leader with interview help from William Rosales. Special thanks to Hannah Thomas, who helped conceive the project and managed it for several years; Alexis Mann brought it to conclusion with skilled acumen and help from Sara Chaganti, Alexandra Bastien, Allison Stagg, Sunny Thomas, and Alicia Atkinson.

The Experts of Color Network family includes some of the most amazing, talented, supportive, engaged difference makers. They include Kilolo Kijakazi, Darrick Hamilton, Sandy Darity, Anne Price, Maya Rockeymoore, Jim Carr, Dedrick Asante-Muhammed, Gabriela Sandoval, Barbara Robles, jon powell, Angela Glover Blackwell, Benita Melton, Gary Cunningham, and Bill Spriggs. In discussions, meetings, strategizing, and action, the work of this family is central to my thinking and the development of this book.

The Levi Strauss, Annie E. Casey, and Open Society Foundations graciously and generously funded important aspects of this work; as important, they were engaged partners. The Ford Foundation was the first and primary investor in the grand endeavor. While the foundation provided the resources,

Kilolo Kijakazi's vision, support, and strategic wisdom were indispensable in our thinking about how to make the greatest impact. I had the distinct pleasure of working closely with some of the best and strategically savviest policy organizations—PolicyLink, Insight, and Dēmos. Heather McGhee, Tamara Draut, Joe Brooks, Alexandra Bastien, and Anne Price are great leaders and wonderful partners.

The amazing Basic Books team did a superb job. The outstanding editorial guidance of Brian Distelberg, Brandon Proia, and Alex Littlefeld helped develop ideas and raw drafts into an accessible and exciting manuscript. The exquisite copyediting of Collin Tracy and Jen Kelland makes me look like a writer. Special thanks to my agent, Geri Thoma at Writers House, for her wisdom and guidance throughout the whole process, from initial book idea to publisher to marketing.

I imposed the low moments, head in the clouds, and time away from family on Ruth Birnberg and Izak Shapiro. As always, their love and encouragement made this a better book; more importantly, they make my life fuller.

If I do one thing well, it is choosing partners.

NOTES

Notes to Introduction

1   Thomas M. Shapiro, *The Hidden Cost of Being African American: How Wealth Perpetuates Inequality* (New York: Oxford University Press, 2004).

2   The National School Lunch Program serves 31 million school-children daily. Children from families with incomes 130 percent below the poverty line qualify for free, nutritious lunches; children from families with incomes between 130 and 185 percent below the poverty line qualify for subsidized lunches. See "National School Lunch Program," Food and Nutrition Service, http://www.fns.usda.gov/sites/default/files/NSLPFactSheet.pdf.

3   They intend to rent them for extended periods before selling them for a capital gain. That strategy is cutting local families and realtors out of the market. In any case, families cannot compete with all-cash offers by investors. See "Public Safety Center Dedicated; Now Ready to Serve," San Bernardino County, May 10, 2013, http://www.sbcounty.gov/rutherford/report /issues/2013_june/images/rr_pr.pdf.

4   See "New Homes in Riverside/San Bernardino, CA," KB Home, http://www.kbhome.com/new-homes-riverside-san-bernardino -county.

5   "Justice Department Reaches $335 Million Settlement to Resolve Allegations of Lending Discrimination by Countrywide

Financial Corporation," US Department of Justice, updated June 22, 2015, http://www.justice.gov/usao/cac/countrywide.html.

6   "Settlement Agreement," HUD, https://portal.hud.gov/hudportal /documents/huddoc?id=DOC_19719.pdf; "HUD Announces $3.2 Million Settlement Against KB Home," HUD Archives, July 6, 2005, http://archives.hud.gov/news/2005/pr05-093 .cfm; Gretchen Morgensen, "Countrywide Mortgage Devastation Lingers as Ex-Chief Moves On," *New York Times*, June 24, 2016, Sunday Business, 1.

7   Many years later, courts finally settled lawsuits. Stringfellow potentially affects the Chino III groundwater basin, which is used for industrial and agricultural purposes and supplies drinking water for approximately 40,000 residents. Southern California manufacturers, including McDonnell Douglas, Montrose Chemical Corp., General Electric, Northrop, and Rockwell International, had dumped waste into the original quarry. Ken Broder, "State's $60 Million Stringfellow Acid Pits Win in High Court Could Cost Insurers Billions," AllGov California, August 13, 2012, http://www.allgov.com/usa/ca/news/where-is-the -money-going/states_60_million_stringfellow_acid_pits_win _in_high_court_could_cost_insurers_billions?news=762402.

8   Office of the Press Secretary, "Remarks by the President on Economic Mobility," White House, https://www.whitehouse .gov/the-press-office/2013/12/04/remarks-president-economic -mobility.

9   Kathrin Brandmeir et al., *Allianz Global Wealth Report 2015*, Allianz.com, September 2015, https://www.allianz.com/v _1443702256000/media/economic_research/publications /specials/en/AGWR2015_ENG.pdf.

10 Emmanuel Saez and Gabriel Zucman, "Wealth Inequality in the United States Since 1913: Evidence from Capitalized Income Tax Data," National Bureau of Economic Research, Working Paper No. 20625, 2014, http://www.nber.org/papers/w20625.pdf.

11 Ibid.; Neal Gabler, "The Secret Shame of Middle-Class Americans," *Atlantic Monthly*, May 2016, http://www.theatlantic.com /magazine/archive/2016/05/my-secret-shame/476415.

12 Even those theorists and pundits who agree that inequality is everywhere argue over how much of it is natural, inevitable, man-

made, or even productive. Meanwhile, disagreement regarding the extent and impact of inequality still abounds—particularly among those who consider income the primary measure.

13 Some of the best work on understanding the new inequality includes Robert Reich's *Saving Capitalism* (New York: Knopf, 2015) and Joseph Stiglitz's *The Price of Inequality* (New York: W. W. Norton, 2012). Nonetheless, these works largely exclude the race and wealth connection.

14 Susan Jones, "Fed Chair Unsure If Capitalism or Oligarchy Describes the U.S.," CBS, May 8, 2014, http://cbsnews.com /news/article/susan-jones/fed-chair-unsure-if-capitalism-or -oligarchy-describes-us.

15 Thomas Piketty, *Capital in the Twentieth Century* (Cambridge, MA: Harvard University Press, 2014).

16 David Shern, A. Blanch, and S. Steverman, "Impact of Toxic Stress on Individuals and Communities: A Review of the Literature," Mental Health America, September 2014, http://www .mentalhealthamerica.net/sites/default/files/Impact%20of %20Toxic%20Stress%20on%20Individuals%20and%20 Communities-A%20Review%20of%20the%20Literature.pdf.

17 Hannah Thomas et al., "The Web of Wealth: Resiliency and Opportunity or Driver of Inequality?," Institute on Assets and Social Policy, July 2014, https://iasp.brandeis.edu/pdfs/2014 /Web.pdf; Janet Boguslaw et al, "Hard Choices: Navigating the Economic Shock of Unemployment," Pew Charitable Trusts, 2013, http://www.pewtrusts.org/~/media/legacy/uploadedfiles /pcs_assets/2013/empreporthardchoicesnavigatingtheeconomic shockofunemploymentpdf.pdf.

Notes to Chapter One

1 John Hills et al., *Wealth in the UK* (Oxford: Oxford University Press, 2013).

2 Dalton Conley and R. Glauber, "Wealth Mobility and Volatility in Black and White," Center for American Progress, July 2008, https://www.americanprogress.org/issues/economy/report /2008/07/29/4662/wealth-mobility-and-volatility-in-black -and-white.

3   Eleni Karagiannaki, "The Effect of Parental Wealth on Children's
     Outcomes in Early Adulthood," CASE Papers, Centre for Anal-
     ysis of Social Exclusion, LSE Research Online, 2012, http://
     eprints.lse.ac.uk/51292; "Indicators of Educational Equity in the
     United States," Pell Institute, 2015, http://www.pellinstitute.org
     /publications-Indicators_of_Higher_Education_Equity_in_the
     _United_States_45_Year_Report.shtml.

4   James Nazroo, Paola Zaninotto, and Edira Gjonca, "Mortality
     and Healthy Life Expectancy," Institute for Fiscal Studies, 2008,
     http://www.ifs.org.uk/elsa/report08/ch8.pdf.

5   Board of Governors of the Federal Reserve System, "Report
     on the Economic Well-Being of U.S. Households in 2013,"
     US Federal Reserve, 2014, https://www.federalreserve.gov
     /econresdata/2013-report-economic-well-being-us-households
     -201407.pdf.

6   Ibid.

7   Thomas M. Shapiro et al., "The Asset Security and Opportu-
     nity Index," Institute on Assets and Social Policy (IASP), 2009,
     https://iasp.brandeis.edu/pdfs/2009/Asset_Security.pdf.

8   Signe-Mary McKernan and Caroline Ratcliffe, "Asset Building
     for Today's Stability and Tomorrow's Security," Urban Insti-
     tute, 2009, http://www.urban.org/sites/default/files/alfresco
     /publication-pdfs/1001374-Asset-Building-for-Today-s
     -Stability-and-Tomorrow-s-Security.PDF.

9   Shapiro et al., "The Asset Security and Opportunity Index."
     Costs associated with each of these three different types of mo-
     bility investments amount to about $14,000.

10   Emmanuel Saez and Gabriel Zucman, "Wealth Inequality in the
     United States Since 1913: Evidence from Capitalized Income
     Tax Data," National Bureau of Economic Research, Working Pa-
     per No. 20625, 2014, http://www.nber.org/papers/w20625.pdf.

11   Ibid.

12   IASP analysis of "2013 Survey of Consumer Finances," Board
     of Governors of the Federal Reserve System, http://www
     .federalreserve.gov/econresdata/scf/scfindex.htm.

13   Thomas M. Shapiro et al., "The Roots of the Widening Racial
     Wealth Gap: Explaining the Black-White Economic Divide,"
     Institute on Assets and Social Policy (IASP), 2013, http://iasp

.brandeis.edu/pdfs/Author/shapiro-thomas-m/racialwealth
gapbrief.pdf; Signe-Mary McKernan et al., "Less Than Equal:
Racial Disparities in Wealth Accumulation," Urban Institute,
2013,   http://www.urban.org/research/publication/less-equal
-racial-disparities-wealth-accumulation/view/full_report;   Paul
Taylor et al., "Wealth Gaps Rise to Record Highs Between
Whites, Blacks and Hispanics," Pew Research Center, 2011,
http://www.pewsocialtrends.org/2011/07/26/wealth-gaps-rise
-to-record-highs-between-whites-blacks-hispanics; Dalton Conley, *Being Black, Living in the Red: Race, Wealth, and Social Policy
in America* (Berkeley: University of California Press, 1999).

14   Building Strong Families Project, "The Long-Term Effects of
Building Strong Families: A Relationship Skills Education Program for Unmarried Parents," MDRC, November 2012, http://
www.mdrc.org/sites/default/files/bsf_36_mo_impact_exec
_summ_0.pdf.

15   Marco Rubio, "Reclaiming the Land of Opportunity: Conservative Reforms for Combatting Poverty," Marco Rubio US Senator for Florida, http://www.rubio.senate.gov/public/index.cfm
/press-releases?ID=958d06fe-16a3-4e8e-b178-664fc10745bf.

16   Elise Gould, Alyssa Davis, and Will Kimball, "Broad Based Wage
Growth Is a Key Tool in the Fight Against Poverty," Economic
Policy Institute, 2015, http://www.epi.org/publication/broad
-based-wage-growth-is-a-key-tool-in-the-fight-against-poverty.

17   Rakesh Kocchar and Richard Fry, "Wealth Inequality Has Widened Along Racial, Ethnic Lines Since End of Great Recession,"
Pew Research Center, 2014, http://www.pewresearch.org/fact
-tank/2014/12/12/racial-wealth-gaps-great-recession.

18   Tatjana Meschede et al., "Wealth Mobility of Families Rais-
ing Children in the 21st Century," Federal Reserve Bank of St.
Louis, 2015, https://www.stlouisfed.org/~/media/Files/PDFs
/Community%20Development/Econ%20Mobility/Sessions
/MeschedeThomasPaper508.pdf.

19   Lisa A. Keister, "Upward Wealth Mobility: Exploring the Roman
Catholic Advantage," *Social Forces* 85 (2007), https://wealth
inequality.org/content/uploads/2015/10/Keister-Upward-Wealth
-mobility-FINAL2.pdf.

20   Rakesh Kochhar, Richard Fry, and Paul Taylor, "Wealth Gaps

Rise to Record Highs Between Whites, Blacks, Hispanics," Pew Research Center, July 26, 2011, http://www.pewsocialtrends .org/2011/07/26/wealth-gaps-rise-to-record-highs-between -whites-blacks-hispanics.

21   Susan K. Uhran et al., "Pursuing the American Dream: Economic Mobility Across Generations," Pew Charitable Trusts, 2012, http://www.pewtrusts.org/~/media/legacy/uploadedfiles /pcs_assets/2012/PursuingAmericanDreampdf.pdf; Susan K. Uhran, "Moving On Up: Why Do Some Americans Leave the Bottom of the Economic Ladder, but Not Others?," Pew Charitable Trusts, 2013, http://www.pewtrusts.org/~/media/Assets /2013/11/01/MovingOnUppdf.pdf.

22   Urahn et al., "Pursuing the American Dream."

23   Ibid.

24   Dalton Conley and Rebecca Glauber, "Family Background, Race and Labor Market Inequality," *ANNALS of the AAPSS* 605, no. 1 (May 2006).

25   Lisa A. Keister and Stephanie Moller, "Wealth Inequality in the United States," *Annual Review of Sociology* 26 (2000): 63–81.

26   Samuel Bowles and Herbert Gintis, "The Inheritance of Inequality," University of Massachusetts Amherst, July 14, 2002, http:// www.umass.edu/preferen/gintis/intergen.pdf; Thomas M. Shapiro, *The Hidden Cost of Being African American: How Wealth Perpetuates Inequality* (New York: Oxford University Press, 2004).

27   Uhran et al., "Pursuing the America Dream."

28   Ibid.

29   Uhran, "Moving On Up."

30   Tatjana Meschede et al., "Family Achievements? How Wealth Trumps Education Among White and Black College Graduates," Federal Reserve Bank of St. Louis, June 2016, https://www .stlouisfed.org/~/media/Files/PDFs/HFS/20160525/slides /Meschede-Shapiro.pdf; Shapiro, "Roots of the Widening Racial Wealth Gap."

31   Signe-Mary McKernan et al., "Impact of the Great Recession and Beyond: Disparities in Wealth Building by Generation and Race," Urban Institute, 2013, http://www.urban.org/research /publication/impact-great-recession-and-beyond.

32   Patrick Sharkey, *Stuck in Place: Urban Neighborhoods and the*

End of Progress Towards Racial Equality (Chicago: University of Chicago Press, 2013).

33 Hannah Thomas et al., "The Web of Wealth: Resiliency and Opportunity or Driver of Inequality?," Institute on Assets and Social Policy, July 2014, https://iasp.brandeis.edu/pdfs/2014/Web.pdf.

34 McKernan et al., "Impact of the Great Recession"; Darrick Hamilton, Austin Algernon, and William Darity Jr., "Whiter Jobs, Higher Wages: Occupational Segregation and the Lower Wages of Black Men," Economic Policy Institute, 2011, http://www.epi.org/publication/whiter_jobs_higher_wages; Hannah Thomas et al., "Employment Capital: How Work Builds and Protects Family Wealth and Security," IASP, December 2013, https://iasp.brandeis.edu/pdfs/2013/Employment.pdf; Thomas M. Shapiro, Tatjana Meschede, and Sam Osoro, "The Widening Racial Wealth Gap: Why Wealth Is Not Color Blind," in *The Assets Perspective: The Rise of Asset Building and Its Impact on Social Policy*, ed. Reid Cramer and Trina R. Williams Shanks (New York: Palgrave Macmillan, 2014); J. C. Henretta, "Parental Status and Child's Homeownership," *American Sociological Review* 49 (1984): 131–140.

35 Barbara A. Butrica and Richard W. Johnson, "Racial, Ethnic, and Gender Differentials in Employer-Sponsored Pensions," Urban Institute, 2010, http://www.urban.org/sites/default/files/alfresco/publication-pdfs/901357-Racial-Ethnic-and-Gender-Differentials-in-Employer-Sponsored-Pensions.PDF.

36 Thomas et al., "The Web of Wealth."

37 G. L. Wallace et al., "Trigger Events and the Financial Outcomes Among Older Households," Center for Financial Security, Working Paper 10-2, 2010, http://www.cfs.wisc.edu/papers/WallaceHavemanHoldenWolfe2010_TriggerPaper.pdf.

38 Christian E. Weller and Jaryn Fields, "The Black and White Labor Gap in America," Center for American Progress, 2011, https://www.americanprogress.org/issues/labor/report/2011/07/25/9992/the-black-and-white-labor-gap-in-america; H. Kim and J. Lee, "Unequal Effects of Elders' Health Problems on Wealth Depletion Across Race and Ethnicity," *Journal of Consumer Affairs* 39 (2015): 148–172.

39 McKernan and Ratcliffe, "Asset Building for Today's Stability and Tomorrow's Security."

40 Durrie Bouscaren, "Cuts in Store for Many of Missouri's Public Assistance Programs," St. Louis Public Radio, June 23, 2015.

41 "Chart Book: SNAP Helps Struggling Families Put Food on the Table," Center on Budget and Policy Priorities, last updated March 24, 2016, http://www.cbpp.org/research/food-assistance /chart-book-snap-helps-struggling-families-put-food-on-the -table.

42 Arloc Sherman and Danilo Trisi, "Deep Poverty Among Children Worsened in the Welfare Law's First Decade," Center on Budget and Policy Priorities, July 23, 2014, http://www .cbpp.org/research/deep-poverty-among-children-worsened-in -welfare-laws-first-decade.

Notes to Chapter Two

1   "2014 Profile of Home Buyers and Sellers," National Association of Realtors, 2014, http://www.realtor.org/sites/default /files/reports/2014/2014-profile-of-home-buyers-and-sellers -highlights.pdf.

2   Heather Taylor and Jing Fu, "Characteristics of Home Buyers," *Housing Economics Special Studies*, National Association of Home Builders, July 1, 2015, updated November 3, 2015, https://www.nahbclassic.org/generic.aspx?sectionID=734 &genericContentID=246591&channelID=311; "Fewer Home Buyers Turn to the Bank of Mom and Dad," MarketWatch, October 28, 2015, http://www.marketwatch.com/story/fewer -homebuyers-are-tapping-their-parents-for-money-2015-10-28; Hispanic home owners receive the largest percentage.

3   Wealth also is required for apartment rentals—typically at least a full first and last month's rent, plus security and pet deposits, as well as move-in, cleaning, and other fees. Although great variability by state and neighborhood exists, the typical monthly rent in 2016 was about $1,300 for a two-bedroom apartment. For example, in St. Louis the median rent for a two-bedroom apartment was a little over $1,000, while in Los Angeles the same-size apartment went for $2,700.

4   Patrick Sharkey, *Stuck in Place: Urban Neighborhoods and the End of Progress Towards Racial Equality* (Chicago: University of Chicago Press, 2013).

5   Hannah Thomas et al., "Location, Location, Location: The Role Neighborhoods Play in Family Wealth and Well-Being," IASP, 2014, https://iasp.brandeis.edu/pdfs/2014/Location.pdf; Margery Austin Turner, Austin Nichols, and Jennifer Comey, "Benefits of Living in High Opportunity Neighborhoods," Urban Institute, September 7, 2012, http://www.urban.org/research /publication/benefits-living-high-opportunity-neighborhoods.

6   Robert J. Sampson, "Neighborhood Effects, Causal Mechanisms, and the Social Structure of the City," in *Analytical Sociology and Social Mechanisms*, ed. Pierre Demeulenaere (Cambridge: Cambridge University Press, 2011), 227–250.

7   Achmat Dangor, *Kafka's Curse* (New York: Vintage, 2000).

8   Jason Purnell, Gabriela Camberos, and Robert Fields, "For the Sake of All," Institute for Public Health, September 20, 2013, https://publichealth.wustl.edu/projects/sake.

9   Walker Moskop, "Searchable Database: 2014 Missouri MAP Scores," *St. Louis Today*, August 29, 2014, http://www.stltoday .com/news/local/stl-info/searchable-database-missouri -map-scores/html_540b5bbf-4cc9-5f74-9087-0cf419966421 .html?appSession=215136101601477; "Metro Academic and Classical High School," *U.S. News*, last updated 2014, http:// www.usnews.com/education/best-high-schools/missouri /districts/st-louis-public-schools/metro-academic-and-classical -high-school-11941.

10 Elisa Crouch, "Three St. Louis Schools, 134 Jobs Face Budget Ax," *St. Louis Post-Dispatch*, February 28, 2013, http://www .stltoday.com/news/local/education/three-st-louis-schools -jobs-face-budget-ax/article_2203e756-a63a-5178-ac3c -4d53d615463c.html.

11 Thomas et al., "Location, Location, Location."

12 Paul Kiel and Annie Waldman, "The Color of Debt: How Collection Suits Squeeze Black Neighborhoods," *ProPublica*, October 8, 2015, https://www.propublica.org/article/debt-collection -lawsuits-squeeze-black-neighborhoods.

13 Thomas et al., "Location, Location, Location."

14 Elizabeth Kneebone, "The Growth and Spread of Concentrated Poverty, 2000 to 2008–2012," Brookings Institute, July 31, 2014, http://www.brookings.edu/research/interactives/2014/concentrated-poverty#/M10420.

15 Joe Cortright and Dillon Mahmoudi, "Lost in Place," *City Observatory*, 2014, http://cityobservatory.org/lost-in-place.

16 Ibid.

17 Patrick Sharkey and Bryan Graham, "Mobility and the Metropolis," Pew Charitable Trusts, 2013, http://www.pewtrusts.org/~/media/legacy/uploadedfiles/pcs_assets/2013/mobilityandthemetropolispdf.pdf.

18 One measure of high-opportunity neighborhoods would include those in the top third of the median family-income distribution among all US census tracts in 2010. Thomas et al., "Location, Location, Location."

19 Mary Pattillo-McCoy, *Black Picket Fences: Privilege and Peril Among the Black Middle Class* (Chicago: University of Chicago Press, 2000).

20 Thomas et al., "Location, Location, Location."

21 Cortright and Mahmoudi, "Lost in Place."

22 Heather Perlberg and John Gittelsohn, "Big Bulk Purchase of U.S. Homes Said to Include St. Louis Properties," *St. Louis Today*, June 10, 2015, http://www.stltoday.com/business/local/big-bulk-purchase-of-u-s-homes-said-to-include/article_a9343d91-048c-58e3-b83a-5e4bda68e4bc.html.

23 Tim Logan and Kevin Crowe, "Foreclosures Start Vicious Sales Circle[;] Buyers Get in and Out Quickly as Homes Crumble," *St. Louis Today*, April 19, 2009, http://www.stltoday.com/news/foreclosures-start-vicious-sales-circle-buyers-get-in-and-out/article_a1e210c8-01e7-5196-8022-4999ad74246a.html.

24 John Gittelsohn and Heather Perlberg, "Blackstone's Home Buying Binge Ends as Prices Surge: Mortgages," *Bloomberg*, March 14, 2014, http://www.bloomberg.com/news/articles/2014-03-14/blackstone-s-home-buying-binge-ends-as-prices-surge-mortgages.

25 Sharkey and Graham, "Mobility."

26 Ibid.

27 Matthias Gafni, "Orinda: District Hires Private Investiga-

tor, Kicks Live-In Nanny's Daughter Out of School," *Eastbay Times*, November 26, 2014, http://www.contracostatimes.com /breaking-news/ci_27024372/orinda-district-hires-private -investigator-kicks-live-nannys.

28 "Orinda Home Values and Prices," Zillow, accessed December 2014, http://www.zillow.com/orinda-ca/home-values.

29 Tricia Rose, "Public Tales Wag the Dog: Telling Stories About Structural Racism in the Post–Civil Rights Era," *Du Bois Review: Social Science Research on Race* 10, no. 2 (2013): 447–469.

30 Caaminee Pandit and Philip Tegeler, "Residential Preferences and Residential Segregation: A Research Overview," Poverty and Race Research Action Council, August 2010, http://www .prrac.org/pdf/PRRAC_Residential_Preferences.pdf.

31 See the Ferguson Commission's report, "Forward Through Ferguson: A Path Toward Racial Equity," at http://forward throughferguson.org/report/executive-summary; "Justice Department Announces Findings of Two Civil Rights Investigations in Ferguson, Missouri," Department of Justice, March 4, 2015, https://www.justice.gov/opa/pr/justice-department-announces -findings-two-civil-rights-investigations-ferguson-missouri.

32 James H. Carr and Archana Pradham, "Analyzing Foreclosures Among High-Income Black/African American and Hispanic/ Latino Borrowers in Prince George's County, Maryland," *Housing and Society* 39, no. 1 (2012): 1–28.

33 Debbie G. Bocian, Wei Li, and Keith S. Ernst, "Foreclosures by Race and Ethnicity: The Demographics of a Crisis," Center for Responsible Lending, June 18, 2010, http://www.responsible lending.org/mortgage-lending/research-analysis/foreclosures -by-race-and-ethnicity.pdf.

34 "Annual Operating Budget: Fiscal Year 2013–2014," City of Ferguson, 2013, http://www.fergusoncity.com/DocumentCenter /View/1609.

Notes to Chapter Three

1 Thomas E. Perez and Erica L. Groshen, "National Compensation Survey: Employee Benefits in the United States, March 2014," US Bureau of Labor Statistics, 2014, http://www.bls.gov

/ncs/ebs/benefits/2014/ebbl0055.pdf; Elise Gould, "Rich People Have Paid Sick Days. Poor People Do Not," Economic Policy Institute, January 21, 2015, http://www.epi.org/publication/rich-people-have-paid-sick-days-poor-people-do-not; Hannah Thomas et al., "Employment Capital: How Work Builds and Protects Family Wealth and Security," IASP, December 2013, https://iasp.brandeis.edu/pdfs/2013/Employment.pdf.

2   "The Lost Decade of the Middle Class: Fewer, Poorer, Gloomier," Pew Research Center, August 22, 2012, http://www.pew socialtrends.org/2012/08/22/the-lost-decade-of-the-middle-class.

3   "The Lost Decade of the Middle Class"; Rakesh Kochhar and Richard Fry, "The American Middle Class Is Losing Ground," Pew Research Center, December 9, 2015, http://www.pewsocial trends.org/files/2015/12/2015-12-09_middle-class_FINAL -report.pdf.

4   Tamara Draut, Jennifer Wheary, and Thomas M. Shapiro, "By a Thread: The New Experience of America's Middle Class," Dēmos, November 28, 2007, http://www.demos.org/publication /thread-new-experience-americas-middle-class.

5   W. Elliot, "Small-Dollar Children's Savings Accounts and Children's College Outcomes," *Children and Youth Services Review* 35, no. 3 (2013): 572–585.

6   Clare O'Connor, "Report: Walmart Workers Cost Taxpayers $6.2 Billion in Public Assistance," *Forbes*, April 15, 2014, http://www.forbes.com/sites/clareoconnor/2014/04/15/report -walmart-workers-cost-taxpayers-6-2-billion-in-public-assistance.

7   Anne Wren, *The Political Economy of the Service Transition* (Oxford: Oxford University Press, 2013).

8   Ibid. See, for example, Lawrence F. Katz and Claudia Goldin, *The Race Between Education and Technology* (Cambridge, MA: Belknap Press, 2010); Lawrence Mishel et al., *The State of Working America* (Ithaca, NY: ILR Press, 2012); Bennett Harrison and Barry Bluestone, *The Great U-turn: Corporate Restructuring and the Polarizing of America* (New York: Perseus Books Group, 1990); Bennett Harrison and Barry Bluestone, *The Deindustrialization of America* (New York: Perseus Books Group, 1982).

9   Carmen DeNavas-Walt and Bernadette D. Proctor, "Income and Poverty in the United States: 2013," US Census Bureau, 2014,

http://www.census.gov/content/dam/Census/library/publications
/2014/demo/p60-249.pdf.

10 "The Low-Wage Recovery and Growing Inequality," National
Employment Law Project, 2012, http://nelp.org/content
/uploads/2015/03/LowWageRecovery2012.pdf.

11 "The Distribution of Household Income and Federal Taxes,
2011," Congressional Budget Office, last modified November
2014,   https://www.cbo.gov/sites/default/files/113th-congress
-2013-2014/reports/49440-Distribution-of-Income-and-Taxes
.pdf; Chad Stone, "A Guide to Statistics on Historical Trends
in Income Inequality," Center on Budget and Policy Priorities,
October 26, 2015, http://www.cbpp.org/research/poverty-and
-inequality/a-guide-to-statistics-on-historical-trends-in
-income-inequality; Elise Gould, "Why America's Workers
Need Faster Wage Growth—and What We Can Do About It,"
Economic Policy Institute, August 27, 2014, http://www.epi.org
/publication/why-americas-workers-need-faster-wage-growth.

12 Ellen R. McGrattan and Richard Rogerson, "Changes in the
Distribution of Family Hours Worked Since 1950," Federal Reserve Bank of Minneapolis, Research Department Staff Report
397, April 2008, https://www.minneapolisfed.org/research/SR
/SR397bw.pdf.

13 "Labor Force Characteristics by Race and Ethnicity, 2013,"
US Bureau of Labor Statistics, August 2014, http://www.bls
.gov/opub/reports/race-and-ethnicity/archive/race_ethnicity
_2013.pdf.

14 Laura Sullivan et al., "The Racial Wealth Gap: Why Policy Matters," Dēmos, 2015, http://www.demos.org/sites/default/files
/publications/RacialWealthGap_1.pdf.

15 Anthony P. Carnevale, Stephen J. Rose, and Ban Cheah, "The
College Payoff," Georgetown University Center on Education and the Workforce, 2011, https://cew.georgetown.edu
/wp-content/uploads/2014/11/collegepayoff-summary.pdf.

16 Thomas M. Shapiro et al., "The Roots of the Widening Racial
Wealth Gap: Explaining the Black-White Economic Divide,"
Institute on Assets and Social Policy (IASP), 2013, http://iasp
.brandeis.edu/pdfs/Author/shapiro-thomas-m/racialwealthgap
brief.pdf.

17   "The Employment Situation—October 2014," US Bureau of
      Labor Statistics, November 7, 2014, http://www.bls.gov/news
      .release/archives/empsit_11072014.pdf; Hannah Thomas et al.,
      "Keeping Dreams Alive: The Lane-Changer Costs of Financial
      Disruptions," IASP, 2014, https://iasp.brandeis.edu/pdfs/2014
      /Lane-Changer.pdf.
18   "Labor Force Characteristics by Race and Ethnicity, 2013."
19   Thomas et al., "Keeping Dreams Alive."
20   Kenneth A. Couch and Robert Fairlie, "Last Hired, First Fired?
      Black-White Unemployment and the Business Cycle," *Demogra-
      phy* 47, no. 1 (2010): 227–247.
21   Algernon Austin, "Whiter Jobs, Higher Wages: Occupational
      Segregation and the Lower Wages of Black Men," Economic Pol-
      icy Institute, February 25, 2011, http://www.epi.org/publication
      /whiter_jobs_higher_wages.
22   William Sites and Virginia Parks, "What Do We Really Know
      About Racial Inequality? Labor Markets, Politics, and the His-
      torical Basis of Black Economic Fortunes," *Politics and Society*
      39, no. 1 (2011): 40–73.
23   Marianne Bertrand and Sendhil Mullainathan, "Are Emily and
      Greg More Employable Than Lakisha and Jamal? A Field Ex-
      periment on Labor Market Discrimination," *American Economic
      Review* 94 (2004): 991–1013. The research evidence regarding
      contemporary employment discrimination is robust and com-
      pelling. The Bertrand and Mullainathan piece is one of many
      studies.
24   Devah Pager, B. Western, and N. Sugie, "Sequencing Disadvan-
      tage: Barriers to Employment Facing Young Black and White
      Men with Criminal Records," *Annals of American Political Sci-
      ence* 623, no. 1 (2009): 195–213.
25   This is consistent with Michelle Alexander's pathbreaking book
      The New Jim Crow (New York: New Press, 2012).
26   Nancy DiTomaso, *The American Non-dilemma: Racial Inequality
      Without Racism* (New York: Russell Sage Foundation, 2013).
27   "Income of the Aged Chartbook, 2012," Social Security Ad-
      ministration, No. 13-11727, 2014, https://www.ssa.gov/policy
      /docs/chartbooks/income_aged/2012/iac12.pdf; "Income of
      the Population 55 or Older, 2012," Social Security Adminis-

tration, No. 13-11871, 2014, https://www.ssa.gov/policy/docs
/statcomps/income_pop55/2012/incpop12.pdf, 234, 239.

28   Larry DeWitt, "Research Note #1: Origins of the Three-Legged
     Stool Metaphor for Social Security," SSA Historian's Office,
     May 1996, https://www.ssa.gov/history/stool.html; Nari Rhee,
     "Race and Retirement Insecurity in the United States," National
     Institute on Retirement Security, December 2013, http://www
     .giaging.org/documents/NIRS_Report_12-10-13.pdf.

29   Alicia H. Munnell, "401(K)/IRA Holdings in 2013: An Up-
     date from the SCF," Center for Retirement Research at Boston
     College, Issue in Brief no. 14-15 (2014), http://crr.bc.edu/wp
     -content/uploads/2014/09/IB_14-15.pdf.

30   Ibid.

31   "Nine Charts About Wealth Inequality in America," Ur-
     ban Institute, March 2015, http://apps.urban.org/features
     /wealth-inequality-charts.

32   Moshe Semyonov, Noah Lewin-Epstein, and William P. Bridges,
     "Explaining Racial Disparities in Access to Employment Bene-
     fits," *Racial and Ethnic Studies* 34, no. 12 (2011): 2069–2095.

33   "401(k) Plans in Living Color: A Study of 401(k) Savings Dis-
     parities Across Racial and Ethnic Groups," Ariel Investments,
     2012, https://www.arielinvestments.com/images/stories/PDF
     /arielhewittstudy_finalweb_7.3.pdf.

34   Ibid.

35   Tatjana Meschede et al., "Family Achievements? How Wealth
     Trumps Education Among White and Black College Graduates,"
     Federal Reserve Bank of St. Louis, June 2016, https://www
     .stlouisfed.org/~/media/Files/PDFs/HFS/20160525/slides
     /Meschede-Shapiro.pdf.

36   David Brooks, "The Cost of Relativism," *New York Times*, March
     10, 2015, http://www.nytimes.com/2015/03/10/opinion/david
     -brooks-the-cost-of-relativism.html.

Notes to Chapter Four

1   Daren Blomquist, "Average Down Payment Drops to Three-
     Year Low of 14.8 Percent for U.S. Home Purchased in
     the First Quarter," RealtyTrac, June 3, 2015, http://www

.realtytrac.com/news/home-prices-and-sales/q1-2015-u-s
-home-purchase-down-payment-report.

2   Colin Gordon, *Mapping Decline: St. Louis and the Fate of the American City* (Philadelphia: University of Pennsylvania Press, 2008).

3   In adjusted 2015 dollars.

4   Ngina Chiteji and Frank Stafford, "Portfolio Choices of Parents and Their Children as Young Adults: Asset Accumulation by African American Families," *American Economic Review* 89, no. 2 (1999): 377–380; William G. Gale and John Karl Scholz, "Intergenerational Transfers and the Accumulation of Wealth," *Journal of Economic Perspectives* 8, no. 4 (1994): 145–160; Mark Wilhelm, "The Role of Intergenerational Transfers in Spreading Asset Ownership," in *Assets for the Poor: The Benefits of Spreading Asset Ownership*, ed. Thomas M. Shapiro and Edward N. Wolff (New York: Russell Sage Foundation, 2001), 132–161.

5   Hannah Thomas et al., "The Web of Wealth: Resiliency and Opportunity or Driver of Inequality?," Institute on Assets and Social Policy, July 2014, https://iasp.brandeis.edu/pdfs/2014/Web.pdf.

6   Ibid.; Signe-Mary McKernan et al., "Private Transfers, Race, and Wealth," Urban Institute, 2011, http://www.urban.org/sites/default/files/alfresco/publication-pdfs/412371-Private-Transfers-Race-and-Wealth.PDF; Wilhelm, "Role of Intergenerational Transfers."

7   Thomas et al., "Web of Wealth"; in 2011 dollars, median only of those receiving inheritance.

8   Author's calculations from Jeffrey P. Thompson and Gustavo A. Suarez, "Exploring the Racial Wealth Gap Using the Survey of Consumer Finances" (paper presented at the Finance and Economics Discussion Series 2015-076, Federal Reserve Board of Governors, Washington, DC, 2015).

9   Thomas et al., "Web of Wealth."

10 McKernan et al., "Private Transfers."

11 Ibid.

12 William R. Emmons and Bryan J. Noeth, "Why Didn't Higher Education Protect Hispanics and Black Wealth?," *In the Balance* 12 (2015), https://www.stlouisfed.org/publications/in-the

-balance/issue12-2015/why-didnt-higher-education-protect-hispanic-and-black-wealth. This analysis uses the Survey of Consumer Finances.

13 Tatjana Meschede et al., "Family Achievements? How Wealth Trumps Education Among White and Black College Graduates," Federal Reserve Bank of St. Louis, June 2016, https://www.stlouisfed.org/~/media/Files/PDFs/HFS/20160525/slides/Meschede-Shapiro.pdf.

14 K. Jack Bauer, *The Mexican War, 1846–1848* (New York: Macmillan, 1974).

15 Tuition information pulled from "Systemwide Information: The CSU's Value to Students," California State University, last updated May 3, 2016, http://www.calstate.edu/value/systemwide.

16 Zillow estimate, Zillow.com, retrieved July 29, 2015.

17 Margaret Cahalan and Laura Perna, "Indicators of Higher Education Equity in the United States," Pell Institute, 2015, http://www.pellinstitute.org/downloads/publications-Indicators_of_Higher_Education_Equity_in_the_US_45_Year_Trend_Report.pdf.

Notes to Chapter Five

1 See Robert Reich, *Saving Capitalism* (New York: Knopf, 2015); Joseph Stiglitz, *The Price of Inequality* (New York: W. W. Norton, 2012); Joseph Stiglitz, *Rewriting the Rules of the American Economy: An Agenda for Growth and Shared Prosperity* (New York: W. W. Norton, 2015); David Cay Johnston, *Free Lunch: How the Wealthiest Americans Enrich Themselves at Government Expense (and Stick You with the Bill)* (New York: Portfolio Publishing, 2012).

2 With homage to Richard Titmuss and his notion of the "iceberg phenomena of social welfare." See Richard Titmuss, "The Role of Redistribution in Social Policy," in *Commitment to Welfare* (New York: Pantheon Books, 1968), 192; Susan Suzanne Mettler, *The Submerged State* (Chicago: University of Chicago Press, 2011); Christopher Howard, *The Hidden Welfare State* (Princeton, NJ: Princeton University Press, 1999).

3 Marc-Andre Gagnon and Sidney Wolfe, "Mirror, Mirror on the

Wall: Medicare Part D Pays Needlessly High Brand-Name Drug Prices Compared with Other OECD Countries and with U.S. Government Programs," Carlton University School of Public Policy and Administration, Policy Brief, July 23, 2015, http://carleton.ca/sppa/wp-content/uploads/Mirror-Mirror-Medicare-Part-D-Released.pdf.

4 Johnston, *Free Lunch*.

5 Daniel R. Levinson, "Concerns with Rebates in the Medicare Part D Program," Department of Health and Human Services, March 2011, http://oig.hhs.gov/oei/reports/oei-02-08-00050.pdf; Gagnon and Wolfe, "Mirror, Mirror."

6 Olga Pierce, "Medicare Drug Planners Now Lobbyists, with Billions at Stake," *ProPublica*, October 20, 2009, https://www.propublica.org/article/medicare-drug-planners-now-lobbyists-with-billions-at-stake-1020; Bruce Bartlett, "Republican Deficit Hypocrisy," *Forbes*, November 20, 2009, http://www.forbes.com/2009/11/19/republican-budget-hypocrisy-health-care-opinions-columnists-bruce-bartlett.html.

7 Philip Mattera and Kasia Tarczynska, "Uncle Sam's Favorite Corporations," Good Jobs First, March 2015, http://www.goodjobsfirst.org/sites/default/files/docs/pdf/UncleSamsFavoriteCorporations.pdf; Staff of the Joint Committee on Taxation, "Estimates of Federal Tax Expenditures for Fiscal Years 2014–2018," House Committee on Ways and Means and the Senate Committee on Finance, August 5, 2014, https://www.heartland.org/sites/default/files/x-97-14.pdf; David Cay Johnston, *The Fine Print: How Big Companies Use Plain English to Rob You Blind* (New York: Portfolio Publishing, 2012).

8 Trina Shanks, "The Homestead Act: A Major Asset-Building Policy in American History," in *Inclusion in the American Dream*, ed. Michael Sherraden (Oxford: Oxford University Press, 2005).

9 "Historical Census of Housing Tables," US Census Bureau, last modified October 31, 2011, https://www.census.gov/hhes/www/housing/census/historic/owner.html.

10 Edward N. Wolff, "Household Wealth Trends in the United States, 1962–2013: What Happened over the Great Recession?," National Bureau of Economic Research, Working Paper 20733, December 2014, http://www.nber.org/papers/w20733;

Thomas M. Shapiro et al., "The Roots of the Widening Racial Wealth Gap: Explaining the Black-White Economic Divide," Institute on Assets and Social Policy (IASP), 2013, http://iasp .brandeis.edu/pdfs/Author/shapiro-thomas-m/racialwealth gapbrief.pdf.

11   "Flow Funds, Balance Sheets, and Integrated Macroeconomic Accounts," Table B.1 in Board of Governors of the Federal Reserve System, September 18, 2015, http://www.federalreserve .gov/releases/z1/20150918/z1.pdf, 101.

12   "Freddie Mac Update," Freddie Mac, November 2015, http:// www.freddiemac.com/investors/pdffiles/investor-presentation .pdf.

13   Gretchen Morgenson, "A Revolving Door Helps Big Banks' Quiet Campaign to Muscle Out Fannie and Freddie," *New York Times*, December 7, 2015, http://www.nytimes.com/2015/12/07 /business/a-revolving-door-helps-big-banks-quiet-campaign-to -muscle-out-fannie-and-freddie.html.

14   Robert Dietz and Donald Haurin, "The Social and Private Micro-Level Consequences of Homeownership," *Journal of Urban Economics* 54 (2003): 401–450.

15   Staff of the Joint Committee on Taxation, "Estimates of Federal Tax."

16   "Policy Basics: Federal Tax Expenditures," Center on Budget and Policy Priorities, February 23, 2016, http://www.cbpp.org /research/federal-tax/policy-basics-federal-tax-expenditures.

17   Robert Collinson, Ingrid G. Ellen, and Jens Ludwig, "Low-Income Housing Policy," National Bureau of Economic Research, Working Paper No. 21071, April 2015, http://www.nber .org/papers/w21071.

18   Benjamin Harris et al., "Tax Subsidies for Asset Development: An Overview and Distribution Analysis," Urban Institute, March 7, 2014, http://www.urban.org/research/publication /tax-subsidies-asset-development-overview-and-distributional -analysis.

19   Adam J. Cole, Geoffrey Gee, and Nicholas Turner, "The Distributional and Revenue Consequences of Reforming the Mortgage Interest Deduction," *National Tax Journal* 64, no. 4 (2011): 977–1000.

20 Other perverse incentives in the current mortgage interest deduction include front-ending allowable interest deductions, creating a tax incentive to sell homes more quickly.

21 Staff of the Joint Committee on Taxation, "Estimates of Federal Tax."

22 Harris et al., "Tax Subsidies."

23 Staff of the Joint Committee on Taxation, "Estimates of Federal Tax."

24 Ibid.

25 Benjamin Harris and Lucie Parker, "The Mortgage Interest Deduction Across Zip Codes," Urban-Brookings Tax Policy Center, December 4, 2014, https://www.brookings.edu/research/the-mortgage-interest-deduction-across-zip-codes.

26 Harris et al., "Tax Subsidies."

27 Ibid.

28 John Sides, "Stories, Science, and Public Opinion About the Estate Tax," George Washington University Department of Political Science, 2011, http://home.gwu.edu/~jsides/estatetax.pdf.

29 Sides, "Stories, Science, and Public Opinion."

30 "Billionaires' Bluff: How America's Richest Families Hide Behind Small Businesses and Family Farms in Effort to Repeal Estate Tax," Public Citizen, June 25, 2015, http://www.citizen.org/documents/billionaires-bluff-estate-tax-report.pdf.

31 David Cay Johnston, "Talk of Lost Farms Reflects Muddle of Estate Tax," New York Times, April 8, 2001, http://www.nytimes.com/2001/04/08/us/talk-of-lost-farms-reflects-muddle-of-estate-tax-debate.html; David Cay Johnston, "No, the Estate Tax Isn't Destroying Family Farms," Aljazeera America, March 27, 2015, http://america.aljazeera.com/opinions/2015/3/the-estate-tax-isnt-destroying-family-farms.html.

32 Staff of the Joint Committee on Taxation, "History, Present Law, and Analysis of the Federal Wealth Transfer Tax System," Joint Committee on Taxation, JCX-52-15, March 16, 2015, https://www.jct.gov/publications.html?func=showdown&id=4744.

33 Susan Harley, "Who Is Behind the Push to Repeal the Estate Tax?," The Hill, July 8, 2015, http://thehill.com/blogs/congress-blog/economy-budget/247111-who-is-behind-the-push-to-repeal-the-estate-tax; "Billionaires' Bluff."

34   The Mars, Wegman, Cos, Taylor, Van Andel, DeVos, Bass, Schwab, and Hall families, for example, actively contribute to lobbying and public campaign efforts. See Harley, "Who Is Behind the Push to Repeal the Estate Tax?" The Koch brothers' efforts went through the 60 Plus Association, whose priorities include privatizing Social Security and killing the estate tax.

35   Staff of the Joint Committee on Taxation, "History, Present Law, and Analysis of the Federal Wealth Transfer Tax System."

36   Ibid.

37   See Martin Feldstein, "Kill the Death Tax Now," *Wall Street Journal*, July 14, 2000, http://www.nber.org/feldstein/wj071400. html; Ryan Ellis, "Top Ten Reasons the U.S. House Will Kill the Death Tax," *Forbes*, April 15, 2015, http://www.forbes.com /sites/ryanellis/2015/04/14/top-ten-reasons-the-u-s-house-will -kill-the-death-tax/2/#358a798933f6.

38   Michael Greenstone et al., "Thirteen Economic Facts About Social Mobility and the Role of Education," Brookings Institution, June 2013, http://www.brookings.edu/research/reports /2013/06/13-facts-higher-education.

39   Harry S. Truman, "Statement by the President Making Public a Report of the Commission on Higher Education," American Presidency Project, December 15, 1947, http://www.presidency .ucsb.edu/ws/index.php?pid=12802; Steven Brint and Jerome Karabel, *The Diverted Dream* (Oxford: Oxford University Press, 1991).

40   Phil Oliff et al., "Recent Deep State Higher Education Cuts May Harm Students and the Economy for Years to Come," Center on Budget and Policy Priorities, March 19, 2013, http://www .cbpp.org/research/recent-deep-state-higher-education-cuts -may-harm-students-and-the-economy-for-years-to-come.

41   "Indicators of Higher Education Equity in the United States—45 Year Trend Report," Pell Institute, 2015, http://www.pell institute.org/downloads/publications-Indicators_of_Higher _Education_Equity_in_the_US_45_Year_Trend_Report.pdf.

42   Laura Sullivan et al., "Less Debt, More Equity: Lowering Student Debt While Closing the Racial Wealth Gap," IASP, November 24, 2015, https://iasp.brandeis.edu/pdfs/2015/lessdebt.pdf.

43   Felix Salmon, "Universities Shouldn't Be Tax Exempt," *Reuters*,

July 8, 2013, http://blogs.reuters.com/felix-salmon/2013/07/08
/universities-shouldnt-be-tax-exempt; Jorge Klor de Alva and
Mark Schneider, "Rich Schools, Poor Students: Tapping Large
University Endowments to Improve Student Outcomes," *Nexus
Research*, 2015, http://www.uctv.tv/shows/Rich-Schools-Poor
-Students-Tapping-Large-University-Endowments-to-Improve
-Student-Outcomes-30112. Many universities, such as Stanford,
recognize the public resources they utilize, such as fire and emer-
gency responders, and thus often give back to local communities
in services and/or tuition breaks for local students.

44   De Alva and Schneider, "Rich Schools, Poor Students."
45   Ibid.

Notes to Chapter Six

1   The Institute on Assets and Social Policy publications in the
     Leveraging Mobility Series include Tatjana Meschede et al.,
     "Family Achievements? How Wealth Trumps Education Among
     White and Black College Graduates," Federal Reserve Bank
     of St. Louis, June 2016, https://www.stlouisfed.org/~/media
     /Files/PDFs/HFS/20160525/slides/Meschede-Shapiro.pdf;
     Hannah Thomas et al., "Location, Location, Location: The
     Role Neighborhoods Play in Family Wealth and Well-Being,"
     IASP, 2014, https://iasp.brandeis.edu/pdfs/2014/Location.pdf;
     Hannah Thomas et al., "Keeping Dreams Alive: The Lane-
     Changer Costs of Financial Disruptions," IASP, 2014, https://
     iasp.brandeis.edu/pdfs/2014/Lane-Changer.pdf; Janet Bogu-
     slaw et al., "Hard Choices: Navigating the Economic Shock
     of Unemployment," Pew Charitable Trusts, 2013, http://www
     .pewtrusts.org/~/media/legacy/uploadedfiles/pcs_assets/2013
     /empreporthardchoicesnavigatingtheeconomicshockofun
     employmentpdf.pdf; Tatjana Meschede et al., "Wealth Mobility
     of Families Raising Children in the 21st Century," Federal Reserve
     Bank of St. Louis, 2015, https://www.stlouisfed.org/~/media
     /Files/PDFs/Community%20Development/Econ%20Mobility
     /Sessions/MeschedeThomasPaper508.pdf; Rebecca Loya et al.,
     "Tipping the Scale: How Assets Shape Economic Wellbeing for
     Women and Families," IASP, 2015, https://iasp.brandeis.edu

/pdfs/2015/tipping.pdf; Laura Sullivan et al., "Navigating an Unclear Path: Preparing for Retirement in the 21st Century," IASP, 2015, https://iasp.brandeis.edu/pdfs/2015/LMS6.pdf; Hannah Thomas et al., "The Web of Wealth: Resiliency and Opportunity or Driver of Inequality?," Institute on Assets and Social Policy, July 2014, https://iasp.brandeis.edu/pdfs/2014/Web.pdf; Hannah Thomas et al., "Employment Capital: How Work Builds and Protects Family Wealth and Security," IASP, December 2013, https://iasp.brandeis.edu/pdfs/2013/Employment.pdf; Hannah Thomas et al., "Leveraging Mobility: Building Wealth, Security and Opportunity for Family Well-Being," IASP, 2013, https://iasp.brandeis.edu/pdfs/2013/LM1-building-wealth.pdf.

2   Joseph Stiglitz, *Rewriting the Rules of the American Economy: An Agenda for Growth and Shared Prosperity* (New York: W. W. Norton, 2015).

3   Robert Reich, *Saving Capitalism* (New York: Knopf, 2015).

4   David Stoesz, "The Excluded: An Estimate of the Consequences of Denying Social Security to Agricultural and Domestic Workers" (working paper, Center for Social Development, St. Louis, Missouri, 2016).

5   Survey data continually point to large majorities supporting expansive, inclusive, and even robust economic policies. See "General Social Survey: Chronicling Changes in American Society," AP-NORC Center for Public Affairs Research, 2015, http://www.apnorc.org/projects/Pages/general-social-survey-chronicling-changes-in-american-society.aspx.

6   "Investing in Tomorrow: Helping Families Build Savings and Assets," Annie E. Casey Foundation, January 20, 2016, http://www.aecf.org/resources/investing-in-tomorrow-helping-families-build-savings-and-assets. This work utilized the IASP Racial Wealth Audit.

7   The pathbreaking work of jon powell is critical here. See jon a. powell, "Post-racialism or Targeted Universalism," *Denver Law Review* 86 (2008): 785, http://scholarship.law.berkeley.edu/facpubs/1633.

8   See Rakesh Kocchar and Richard Fry, "Wealth Inequality Has Widened Along Racial, Ethnic Lines Since End of Great Recession," Pew Research Center, 2014, http://www.pewresearch

.org/fact-tank/2014/12/12/racial-wealth-gaps-great-recession; Sarah D. Wolff, "The State of Lending in America and Its Impact on U.S. Households," Center for Responsible Lending, June 2015, http://www.responsiblelending.org/state-of-lending /State-of-Lending-report-1.pdf.

9   The Tax Alliance for Economic Mobility includes the following organizations or leaders associated with these organizations: AARP, Aspen Institute/Initiative on Financial Security, Asset Funders Network, Bend the Arc, Institute on Assets and Social Policy, Center for American Progress, Center for Community Change, Center on Budget and Policy Priorities, Center for Global Policy Solutions, City and County of San Francisco, CLASP, Color of Change, Emory Law School, First Focus, Greenlining Institute, Insight Center for Community Economic Development, Institute for Women's Policy Studies, Leadership Conference on Civil and Human Rights, Massachusetts Budget and Policy Center, National Association for the Advancement of Colored People, National Alliance of Community Economic Development Associations, National Association for Latino Community Asset Builders, National Coalition for Asian Pacific American Community Development, National Council of La Raza, National Urban League, New America Foundation, Oklahoma Native Assets Coalition, PICO National Network, Skadden, Arps, Slate, Meagher & Flom LLP, UCLA Asian American Studies Center, United for a Fair Economy, Washington University in St. Louis, Women Donors Network, United Way Worldwide, Urban Institute, and the Young Invincibles. For the Tax Alliance for Economic Mobility proposal, see Will Fischer and Chye-Ching Huang, "Mortgage Interest Deduction Is Ripe for Reform," Center on Budget and Policy Priorities, June 25, 2013, http://www.cbpp.org/research /mortgage-interest-deduction-is-ripe-for-reform.

10   Benjamin Harris, Eugene Steuerle, and Amanda Eng, "New Perspectives on Homeownership Tax Incentives," Brookings Institute, January 6, 2014, https://www.brookings.edu/research /new-perspectives-on-homeownership-tax-incentives.

11   Karen Dynan, Ted Gayer, and Natasha Plotkin, "The Recent Homebuyer Tax Credit: Evaluation and Lessons for the Future,"

Economic Studies at Brookings, June 28, 2013, http://www
.brookings.edu/~/media/Research/Files/Papers/2013/06/28
%20homebuyer%20tax%20credit%20dynan%20gayer/28
_homebuyer_tax_credit_dynan_gayer.pdf.

12   "Affirmatively Furthering Fair Housing," US Department of
Housing and Urban Development, July 16, 2015, https://www
.huduser.gov/portal/affht_pt.html#final-rule.

13   Raj Chetty, Nathaniel Hendren, and Lawrence F. Katz, "The Effects of Exposure to Better Neighborhoods on Children: New
Evidence from the Moving to Opportunity Experiment," *American Economic Review* 106, no. 4 (April 2016): 855–902.

14   Devah Pager, *Marked: Race, Crime, and Finding Work in an Era of
Mass Incarceration* (Chicago: University of Chicago Press, 2009).

15   Marianne Bertrand and Sendhil Mullainathan, "Are Emily and
Greg More Employable Than Lakisha and Jamal? A Field Ex-
periment on Labor Market Discrimination," *American Economic
Review* 94 (2004): 991–1013.

16   Maya Rockeymoore and Meizhu Lui, *Plan for a New Future: The
Impact of Social Security Reform on People of Color* (Washington,
DC: Commission to Modernize Social Security, 2011), http://
latinosforasecureretirement.org/resources/new_future_social
_security_commission_report_.pdf.

17   "Securing Our Financial Future: Report of the Commission on
Retirement Security and Personal Savings," Bipartisan Policy
Center, June 2016, http://cdn.bipartisanpolicy.org/wp-content
/uploads/2016/06/BPC-Retirement-Security-Report.pdf. See
a dissenting note from commission member Kilolo Kijakazi,
"Why I Chose Not to Endorse the Bipartisan Policy Center
Commission's Retirement Security Report," Urban Institute, June 9, 2016, http://www.urban.org/urban-wire/why
-i-chose-not-endorse-bipartisan-policy-center-commissions
-retirement-security-report. To prevent this revenue shortfall,
the commission recommended tweaking the benefit formula,
gradually increasing the maximum wage to which the payroll
tax is applied, slightly increasing the payroll tax over ten years,
increasing full retirement age by two years, and reducing the
annual cost-of-living adjustment.

18   Laura Sullivan et al., "Less Debt, More Equity: Lowering Student

Debt While Closing the Racial Wealth Gap," IASP, November 24, 2015, https://iasp.brandeis.edu/pdfs/2015/lessdebt.pdf.

19 Estimating the cost of reducing student debt is quite complicated, as it includes policy design, deciding between phase-in and all-at-once implementation, and numerous other assumptions difficult to model. The sum of all student debt exceeds $1.2 trillion. A policy that reduces half the debt of those with incomes less than $25,000 would impact approximately 10 to 15 percent of college graduates. The cost is not small, but the returns would be enormous.

20 W. Elliot, "Small-Dollar Children's Savings Accounts and Children's College Outcomes," *Children and Youth Services Review* 35, no. 3 (2013): 572–585.

21 See William Darity Jr. and Darrick Hamilton, "Bold Policies for Economic Justice," *Review of Black Political Economy* 39, no. 1 (March 2012): 79–85.

22 "Investing in Tomorrow."

23 "2015 EITC Income Limits, Maximum Credit Amounts and Tax Law Updates," Internal Revenue Service, November 24, 2016, https://www.irs.gov/credits-deductions/individuals/earned-income-tax-credit/eitc-income-limits-maximum-credit-amounts; "Policy Basics: The Earned Income Tax Credit," Center on Budget and Policy Priorities, January 15, 2016, http://www.cbpp.org/research/federal-tax/policy-basics-the-earned-income-tax-credit.

24 For simplicity, this basic set of responsible reforms is modeled on Senator Bernie Sanders's proposal, which includes features regarding the valuation of property. A conservative tax advocacy organization, the Tax Foundation, tried to model how much revenue would be generated by such a proposal and reported that about $30 billion in federal revenue would result from such a reformed estate tax. Their assumptions were opaque, so their figure should be taken as a ballpark estimate. Alan Cole and Scott Greenberg, "Details and Analysis of Senator Bernie Sanders's Tax Plan," Tax Foundation, January 2016, http://taxfoundation.org/sites/taxfoundation.org/files/docs/TaxFoundation-FF498.pdf

INDEX

Max Pearlstein

THOMAS M. SHAPIRO is Pokross Professor of Law and Social Policy at the Heller School, Brandeis University, where he directs the Institute on Assets and Social Policy. The author of four books, including *The Hidden Cost of Being African American* and, with Melvin Oliver, *Black Wealth/White Wealth*, he lives in Jamaica Plain, Massachusetts.